School-Based Assessment in a Caribbean Public Examination

School-Based Assessment in a Caribbean Public Examination

Stafford A. Griffith

THE UNIVERSITY OF THE WEST INDIES PRESS
Jamaica • Barbados • Trinidad and Tobago

The University of the West Indies Press
7A Gibraltar Hall Road, Mona
Kingston 7, Jamaica
www.uwipress.com

© Stafford A. Griffith, 2015
All rights reserved. Published 2015

A catalogue record of this book is available from the National Library of Jamaica.

ISBN: 978-976-640-554-0 (print)
978-976-640-563-2 (Kindle)
978-976-640-572-4 (ePub)

Cover design by Robert Harris
Typesetting by The Beget, India

Printed in the United States of America

Contents

List of Abbreviations   vii

Part 1: The History and Context

Chapter 1   CXC as a Caribbean Public Examinations Board   3

Chapter 2   Public Examinations Tailored to Caribbean Needs   13

Chapter 3   Quality Assurance: An Important Role as a Regional Public Examinations Board   23

Chapter 4   Innovations by CXC in the Offer of Public Examinations in the Caribbean   33

Part 2: Key Issues

Chapter 5   Individualizing a Part of the Curriculum through School-Based Assessment   47

Chapter 6   Developing and Assessing Skills Often Excluded from Conventional Public Examinations   57

Chapter 7   The Centrality of Feedback   65

Chapter 8   Summative Assessment of Candidates and the Role of the Teacher   73

Part 3: New Directions

Chapter 9   The Alternative Paper to School-Based Assessment   85

Chapter 10	Group Work in School-Based Assessment	95
Chapter 11	A Single Project for Clusters of Subjects	107
Chapter 12	Adoption of the Benefits of School-Based Assessment through Continuous Assessment	117
References		123
Index		135

Abbreviations

AQA	Assessment and Qualifications Alliance
BGCSE	Bahamas General Certificate of Secondary Education
CAPE	Caribbean Advanced Proficiency Examination
CCSLC	Caribbean Certificate of Secondary Level Competence
CPEA	Caribbean Primary Exit Examination
CSE	Certificate of Secondary Education
CSEC	Caribbean Secondary Education Certificate
CVQ	Caribbean Vocational Qualification
CXC	Caribbean Examinations Council
GCE A Level	General Certificate of Education Advanced Level
GCE O Level	General Certificate of Education Ordinary Level
GCSE	General Certificate of Secondary Education
GSAT	Grade Six Achievement Test
ICT	information and communication technology
IGCSE	International General Certificate of Secondary Education
JWU	Johnson & Wales University
SUBSEC	Sub-Committee of the School Examinations Committee
UK NARIC	UK National Academic Recognition Information Centre

1 | The History and Context

1 | CXC as a Caribbean Public Examinations Board

The First Public Examinations

Biblical accounts in the Old Testament have at times been invoked, in dating the first examinations. It has been suggested that the first examinations were administered in the Garden of Eden (Bruce 1969; Skurnik 1976). There, Adam and Eve were subjected to a simple negative test: they were not to partake of the forbidden fruit. According to Bruce (1969, 1), "only two results were possible, pass or fail, and the examiner was infallible". They failed, and the consequences were severe. From a theological standpoint, man and woman have had to endure the burden of this failure since then.

Another, more frequently cited, biblical account is taken from Judges 12:4–6. This is said to be the first recorded oral examination (Skurnik 1976). Here, a test was devised by the Gileadite army to identify members of the defeated Ephraimite army who were attempting to escape under cover of a false identity. The Gileadites positioned themselves at the passages of Jordan and refused to let anyone pass who could not pronounce the word "shibboleth". It was known that this presented a phonetic difficulty for the Gileadites as they pronounced the word "sibboleth" rather than "shibboleth". Some forty-two thousand Ephraimites failed this examination. They were summarily executed.

The more recent history of public examinations suggests that the direct consequences for those who fail to respond satisfactorily are less grave than those associated with the two biblical accounts. Nevertheless, one may reasonably point to the fact that, even today, the stress associated with the preparation for, and the taking of, some public examinations may have grave consequences for examinees. In some social and cultural environments, the burden of failure may be so heavy to carry that it ultimately proves to be fatal. Because of the awareness of the possible consequences of public examinations for some candidates, a number of measures are often instituted to put them more at ease in preparing for these examinations and in treating with the outcome of their efforts.

Acknowledging the Chinese Legacy in Public Examinations

Outside of the biblical accounts, historians generally agree that the Chinese were the first to use public examinations. These were introduced around 2000 BC to measure the proficiency of candidates for public office and to reduce patronage (Cohen and Wollack 2006; DuBois 1970; Rogers 1995). It is heartening to note the continued acknowledgement of the contribution of the Chinese to the development of examinations in the fourth edition of the authoritative *Educational Measurement*. In 1964, DuBois had found it necessary to state poignantly that the Chinese "invented the psychological test" and to lament that "the prolonged and intensive Chinese experience with testing seems to have been completely ignored by contemporary psychometricians" (DuBois 1966, 29). In considering school-based assessment in a public examination, the author of this book feels an obligation to follow the example of the few books about examinations which have since paid tribute to the Chinese for their contribution to public examinations which now form an essential feature of the education system in many countries across the globe.

By 1115 BC, China had established formal procedures for the examination of candidates for public office. The tests comprising the examination assessed proficiency in six arts: music, archery, horsemanship, writing, arithmetic, and the rites and ceremonies of public and social life. Confucian ethics later became an important part of the process of selecting candidates for these examinations.

By 165 BC, district magistrates were required to send candidates of high moral standing to the capital to be examined. The tests were, by that time, expanded to include not just the six arts but also geography, civil law, military matters, agriculture and revenue administration (DuBois 1966). By the middle of the fourteenth century, these examinations had evolved into a more structured format and focused more on the political administration dimension than on physical prowess (Bowman 1989; Cohen and Wollack 2006; DuBois 1970).

Civil service testing that was later introduced in Europe in the late eighteenth century followed the Chinese model. The modern era of public examinations may be said to have emerged in the middle of the nineteenth century with the development of the British Civil Service examinations used to select trainees for the civil service in

India. Later, the use of the examinations was extended to the selection of civil servants in Britain (Cohen and Wollack 2006; Roach 1971; The World Bank Group 2002a).

In light of this history of public examinations, one needs to read with caution the first words in the first chapter of Roach's publication of *Public Examinations in England, 1850–1900* (1971, 3), which asserts that "public examinations were one of the great discoveries of nineteenth-century Englishmen". This statement may give the erroneous impression that public examinations originated in England. There can be no quarrel with the statement, however, if it seeks to suggest that it was a great moment in history when the English came to know about, or discover, public examinations. That latter meaning may well be intended by Roach, even though this is not obvious.

It is clear that once the English "discovered" public examinations, a number of reforms were initiated in their education system, which saw more open competition for the privileges bestowed by education. This was done through open and competitive examinations and certification. These examinations had various objectives. One was to classify students according to their ability and thus open options for those with higher ability levels by providing the opportunity for advanced studies. A second, somewhat related, but more vocational objective was to determine the fitness of candidates for public office or for an independent profession. A third objective was to provide opportunities for advancement or upward mobility of the less privileged members of the society. The English were no doubt influential in the dissemination of the idea of a public examination across the globe.

A Modern Concept of Public Examinations

Today, public examinations are an important aspect of modern education systems. In discussing the importance of external examinations (essentially public examinations), Heyneman (2009) makes the point that examinations used for monitoring and selection are necessary to all modern nations. Contemporary public examinations have been described as "typically formal, summative, and controlled by an agent external to the school where the student has studied" (World Bank Group 2002a). Key requirements of public examinations are:

1. the examination papers and system of marking should be both valid and reliable;
2. the conduct of the examination should be regarded as fair and should have a high degree of public acceptance;
3. there should be no particular candidate or group of candidates that has an unfair advantage over others;
4. the examination should be administered according to an established schedule;

5. the examination should be open to public scrutiny;
6. the examination should promote good educational practices;
7. the examination services must be delivered efficiently. (World Bank Group 2002a)

The considerations mentioned above are important in a public examination. However, three of these requirements, those relating to (1) the validity and reliability of the examination papers and system of marking, (2) the fairness and public acceptance of the conduct of the examination and (3) assurances that no particular candidate or group of candidates will have an unfair advantage over others, are critical to a public examination. They may be regarded as the essentials of a public examination. In later chapters in this book, these three features will be given further attention as, together, they define the most important technical qualities of a public examination.

However, the need for efficiency in public examinations merits further consideration. It has been cited as an important consideration in public examinations. Kivilu (2004) includes it in the four key characteristics of a public examination, the other three being validity, reliability and acceptability which are related to aspects of the first three requirements noted above. Efficiency refers to a cost-effective implementation of an examination, compared with other ways of getting useful information for relevant decision-making. Kivilu laments that, after forty years of independence, some African countries are still spending scarce resources on foreign examinations boards or on foreign companies for printing examination papers. This, according to the author, calls into question the efficiency of public examinations in those countries.

In the Caribbean, the same complaint cannot be made about spending on foreign examinations boards. It must be acknowledged, though, that the premier examinations board in the region, the Caribbean Examinations Council (CXC), while developing and administering its own examinations, continues to depend on foreign companies to print and package its examination papers. There can be no doubt that this leads to the spending of scarce resources on foreign companies. However, bearing in mind the security concerns that the board seeks to address by printing overseas, the practice could hardly be explained in terms of mere inefficiency.

The lack of confidence in obtaining secure printing services in the region is a critical issue that needs to be addressed. This is an issue with which the region continues to grapple and one which requires resolution. The capacity to provide secure printing services for large-scale public examinations must be developed in the region. This is an area in which CXC may need to take the leadership initiative.

Public Examinations in the Caribbean

It was noted earlier that the first English public examinations were concerned, essentially, with (1) classification of students and identifying those suitable for higher education, (2) determining the fitness of students for certain jobs and (3) providing opportunities for upward social mobility. These notions of the role of public examinations in the education system were transported by the British in the nineteenth century to the colonies which formed the British Empire, including those of the Caribbean. Although most countries of the former British Empire have now developed their own examination systems, these are still patterned after the British model (Bissoondoyal 2004). A few continue to use the examinations of British examinations boards. Sometimes these are specially modified to take local content and other realities into account, but they often exist side by side with other regional or national examinations.

In the Caribbean, the end-of-primary-school examinations, which were initially patterned after the eleven-plus examination of the British education system, have gone through several reforms. However, these eleven-plus examinations, called by various names, remain an essential mechanism in most Caribbean countries for the selection and placement of students into secondary education programmes at the end of primary school. The emphasis is usually on mathematics and language arts, even though some countries include other subjects, mainly science and social studies (Griffith and Jennings-Craig 2010).

At the secondary level, the British examinations of the University of London and the University of Cambridge were extensively used in the former colonies of the Caribbean. More recently, these countries have taken steps to develop their own system of examinations. However, the influence of the British examination system is still evident in these initiatives.

In the Commonwealth of the Bahamas, for example, the Cambridge and London examinations were replaced by a Bahamas General Certificate of Secondary Education (BGCSE) with the assistance of the University of Cambridge Local Examinations Syndicate. The new examinations were introduced in 1993 (Sumner and Archer 1996). The clear continuity of the link with the University of Cambridge is evident in the crest of the University of Cambridge which adorns the certificate, side by side with that of the Commonwealth of the Bahamas. Indeed, in 2009, the Commonwealth of the Bahamas obtained a statement from the University of Cambridge (International Examinations) which indicated that "University of Cambridge International Examinations has taken measures to ensure that the standards of achievement represented by grades A–G in the 2009 BGCSE examination in the subjects listed . . . are equivalent to those represented by the corresponding grades in the International General Certificate of Secondary Education (IGCSE) and the General Certificate of Education O Level (GCE O level)" (Ministry of Education [Bahamas] website 2009).

This statement reflects an obvious effort to sustain the link to the British examinations. Various reasons have been advanced for the type of model adopted by small states such as the Commonwealth of the Bahamas. These include limited local expertise and the need for security in an environment where everyone knows everyone else (Bissoondoyal 2004). However, the most important consideration seems to be the desire to provide secondary school graduates with qualifications that are recognized nationally and internationally and which can therefore be easily accepted for purposes of employment and further study in the national, regional and international community (Bissoondoyal 2004; Crocombe and Crocombe 1994).

A number of former British colonies have adopted a model of regional examinations boards to serve a group of countries. This is exemplified by boards such as the West African Examinations Council and the Caribbean Examinations Council. These examinations boards are modelled after the British boards but serve groups of countries. Because each board serves several member countries, the problems that may be attendant on a single-country board are mitigated. These include those related to small population size and limited pool of expertise. The collective approach also helps to enhance the local, regional and international portability of the qualifications. These boards are able to benefit from the services of specialists drawn from major national and regional educational institutions, including universities, to help in ensuring that the examinations meet internationally acceptable standards for employment in certain fields and for further studies.

The Establishment of a Caribbean Examinations Council

The establishment of CXC was a significant achievement in the region. The council's establishment was influenced by the developments in the 1960s which saw Caribbean territories joining their counterparts in the British Empire in seeking political independence. As part of the effort to establish and consolidate their independence, countries in the region sought to establish institutions that would reflect the interests, character and aspirations of Caribbean people (Griffith 1999).

As early as 19 July 1961, during the period of the short-lived West Indian federation, the Seventh Meeting of the Caribbean Advisory Committee held in Jamaica noted that there was "a unanimous desire among teachers and representatives of ministries of education and education departments for the establishment of a West Indies Examinations Council" (CXC 1975, 1).

A number of important matters related to the establishment of such a council were pursued subsequently, including the form that the proposed council should take and where the headquarters should be located. Similar issues with respect to the West Indian federation had engaged the attention of governments during its brief existence from 1958 to 1962. Inability to resolve matters such as the location of the federal capital had contributed to the wrangling that led to the demise of that federation (CARICOM Secretariat 2005).

Progress in decision-making for the establishment of a Caribbean Examinations Council was understandably slow during the decade following the collapse of the federation in 1962. Every significant step towards the establishment of another regional institution or organization would have had to be carefully considered to avoid the experience of the failed federation.

The establishment of the Caribbean Free Trade Association in 1965 was an important breakthrough. It was another effort to pursue regional integration. As more countries joined the association, a number of issues related to regional integration again occupied the attention of Caribbean governments. In 1970, an education desk was established in the secretariat of the association. Its main responsibility was to identify and coordinate activities for regional cooperation in education. This saw a more intensive engagement with the matter of a regional examinations council. In 1972, this council became a reality (CXC 1975; CARICOM Secretariat 2005).

The "Agreement Establishing the Caribbean Examinations Council" became effective in April 1972, with thirteen Caribbean governments as signatories. These were Antigua and Barbuda, Barbados, Belize, British Virgin Islands, Cayman Islands, Dominica, Grenada, Guyana, Montserrat, St Kitts–Nevis–Anguilla, St Lucia, St Vincent and the Grenadines, and the Turks and Caicos Islands. By April 1973, following an amendment that, inter alia, provided for an administrative and operational centre in Jamaica, two other countries – Jamaica, and Trinidad and Tobago – became signatories to the agreement, bringing the total number of participating countries to fifteen (CXC 1974). With the subsequent withdrawal of the Cayman Islands, the number of participating territories was reduced to fourteen (CXC 1978). It should be noted that, subsequent to the signing of the agreement, political difficulties within the associated state of St Kitts–Nevis–Anguilla led to the withdrawal of Anguilla from the three-island state, and that island temporarily ceased to have its original status with the council.

However, both Anguilla and the Cayman Islands have since returned to the CXC fold. Anguilla did so in 1987 by signing a supplementary agreement, and the Cayman Islands followed suit by signing a similar agreement in 1993. This brought the number of participating territories to sixteen.

It is evident that the Caribbean Examinations Council did not escape the usual vicissitudes of establishing a regional organization to serve the interests of a number of different countries. However, with more and more countries gaining their independence in the wake of the failed federation, and the desire to consolidate that independence, there was renewed interest in an examinations board independent of Britain. Despite the minor adjustments that were made to the membership of the council during the first two decades of its existence, a large majority of members remained with the organization without change, since its inception in 1972. The dedicated work and tenacity of these members guided the organization to the eventual stability of membership it enjoys today. The Caribbean Examinations Council has evolved to become one of the most stable and successful regional organizations of the Caribbean.

An important development in the history of the council was the extension of examination services to the Dutch-speaking territories of Suriname, Saba and St Maarten. All three territories enter students for the CXC examinations.

The CXC Mandate

Article III (a) of the Agreement Establishing the Caribbean Examinations Council (1972) captures the essence of the mandate of the council. Article III (a) charged the council with conducting "such examinations as it may think appropriate" and awarding "certificates and diplomas on the results of the examinations so conducted". The agreement itself set out in detail the duties of the council and the administrative arrangements for its proper functioning.

The discussions among countries in the region since the early 1960s clearly indicated that the council was required to support a new direction in education. It was envisaged that the council would be able to satisfy most of the educational assessment and evaluation needs of the region (CXC 1975). However, it was expected that, initially, "CXC will concentrate on a secondary terminal examination at about the GCE 'O' or equivalent level for students in the 16+ age group" (CXC 1975, 4).

The council's mandate was, clearly, not restricted to the provision of examinations at the secondary level. Rather, the council was mandated to conduct examinations "as it may think appropriate" and "award certificates and diplomas on the results of the examinations conducted". Until recently, much of the work of the council concentrated on end-of-secondary-school examinations. The council has now extended the examination services it provides to other levels of the education system.

The CXC Administrative Arrangements

CXC was challenged to assume responsibility for a new set of examinations that reflected a Caribbean ethos. The establishment of the council responded to a crosssection of interests that went well beyond what may be considered as strictly examination matters. The new board, according to Fergus (1980, 87), "had to be regarded as an agent of fundamental change in education". Up to the 1960s, the secondary education system in the region was dominated by curricula based on foreign examinations. With the advent of the CXC as an examining body in the 1970s, a change was initiated in secondary education that saw modifications in the secondary education curriculum of many countries to establish a firm link to the CXC regional examinations. This led to the gradual Caribbeanization of the secondary curriculum and the realization of an important part of the education reform which countries in the region so eagerly sought in the post-independence era.

CXC was established as a fully managed Caribbean operation, financed mainly by subventions from member territories and examination fees. The administrative arrangements of the council reflect the determination to deal with territorial anxieties linked to the failure of the West Indian federation in the early 1960s and the need for a careful balancing of territorial interests to cope with some of the difficulties inherent in the establishment of a regional organization to serve the interests of several territories. A pragmatic option was pursued which maintained a close relationship with all territories. Also, managerial structures which took into account the geographical location and potential demand for services based on population size were established.

The administrative and operational work of the council is conducted through offices located in the eastern and western zones of the region. The eastern zone office is located in Barbados and houses the headquarters of the council. The registrar, the council's chief executive officer, is based at this office. Most of the technical operations of the council, too, are managed from this office.

The western zone office is located in Jamaica, which is the largest population centre of the region served by the council. It has special responsibilities for syllabus development and maintenance, and related activities. It also provides support for the work of the council in the north-western Caribbean countries in particular. The pro-registrar of the council is based at the western zone office in Jamaica.

The council maintains its administrative links with the respective territories through a national registrar appointed by each of the respective countries as part of the staffing arrangements within ministries or departments of education. In Jamaica, the responsibilities associated with the local registrar are undertaken by a national overseas examinations commission linked to the Ministry of Education. The local registrars provide an important interface between the administrative operations of the council and the national ministries of education. They are responsible for the management of the local operations associated with the administration of the council's examinations.

The CXC interface with participating territories is further strengthened by the work of national committees established by each country. A national committee comprises representatives of the Ministry of Education, the teaching profession, university representatives, and other stakeholders in education. The responsibilities of the committee include advising the council on matters relating to syllabuses and examinations. These committees provide a vital nexus between the CXC technical operations and the users of CXC services in a territory. The national committees have been playing a critical role in the development and progress of CXC since its inception. The ongoing work in which they are involved is vital to the proper functioning of the council.

2 | Public Examinations Tailored to Caribbean Needs

Secondary Level

The Caribbean Examinations Council has taken a number of bold initiatives to respond to the education needs of the region. Most of these initiatives have done well, although a few have had a disappointing response. The council initiated its public examinations process by defining three schemes of examinations under the Caribbean Secondary Education Certificate (CSEC). The three schemes were not merely to replace the General Certificate of Education Ordinary Level (GCE O level) examinations offered in the region by the UK examinations boards: they were also designed to cater to a wider population of students than the GCE O level examinations did.

The UK examinations boards had, in fact, sought to address the issue of an examination that catered to a wider population of students, as recommended by the Beloe report of 1960. In keeping with the recommendations of the report, the Certificate of Secondary Education (CSE) was introduced in 1965. This examination, similar to the GCE O level, was offered to Britain's colonies and former colonies. Though the CSE had an overlapping grade scale with the GCE O level, it catered, essentially, for the 40 per cent of students below the 20 per cent targeted by the GCE O level (AQA 2003). By implication, the bottom 40 per cent of the population was regarded as "unexaminable".

The three schemes of examinations under the CXC CSEC examinations, taken together, considered no such restrictions. In defining the three schemes, no attempt was made, as in the GCE-CSE scheme, to link them to proportions of students at the top or bottom of the achievement scale or to conceptualize the examinations as being beyond the reach of any proportion of candidates.

It was not intended that these three schemes of examinations would separate candidates into three separate groups. Rather, it was intended that they would provide greater flexibility to students in defining a course of study at the upper secondary level that was in keeping with their interests and abilities. The typical CSEC candidate was, therefore, expected to choose a mix of subjects taken under two or three schemes (Griffith 1999).

This attempt to cast the three CSEC schemes as being on an equivalent plane and therefore appropriate for consideration by all students might have contributed to some of the challenges which the council later faced with the schemes and to the council's subsequent decision to develop a complementary examination, the Caribbean Certificate of Secondary Level Competence (CCSLC), which was clearly at the pre-CSEC level.

The three schemes of the CSEC examinations developed by the council were classified as general proficiency, basic proficiency and technical proficiency. This decision to have three schemes under the same examination was perhaps overambitious, and the council subsequently found it necessary to make some adjustments. The distinction between the three schemes at essentially the same level of secondary-education completion was challenging to establish. It proved particularly difficult to distinguish basic proficiency from the other two proficiencies.

According to the council, all three schemes were intended primarily for candidates who had completed five years of secondary education. A general proficiency syllabus and examination was defined as requiring "a sufficient breadth of knowledge and depth of understanding to allow candidates who respond well to undertake study of the specific subject of examination beyond the fifth year of secondary school" (CXC 1991, 5).

This was clear enough and seemed to fit the generally accepted notion of the purpose of the GCE O level examinations which the CSEC would replace. After the usual challenges of confidence-building associated with the introduction of a new examination to replace one with which stakeholders had become familiar, the general proficiency was accepted as the gold standard of secondary school achievement in the region. It remains the primary scheme under which CSEC subjects are offered by the council. In the May–June 2013 examination, thirty-four subjects were offered under this scheme (CXC 2013a).

In seeking to distinguish the basic proficiency from the general proficiency, the council explained that a basic proficiency syllabus and examination catered to the needs of candidates who may not subsequently pursue further studies in areas related to the subject. It was designed to make different cognitive demands on candidates than those made by the general proficiency (CXC 1991).

It appears that the intention was to have a basic proficiency scheme that was less demanding than the general proficiency scheme. However, the council stringently avoided making any statement about the examinations being at different levels and instead sought to present the basic proficiency merely as making cognitive demands which were different from those of the general proficiency. It was difficult to grasp what was intended by having an examination which was premised on the same number of years of schooling as the general proficiency but which supposedly made different cognitive demands on candidates.

In retrospect, it would have been better to present the basic proficiency as a foundation for general proficiency, as a scheme that made a lower level of demand on candidates than general proficiency. The linking of these two schemes through at least a common paper or common set of examination questions further obfuscated the value of basic proficiency as a different examination. Teachers did not perceive the instructional demands for the two proficiencies to be different.

Essentially, the perception of stakeholders was that there was no difference in the nature and level of demand of the basic proficiency, compared with the general proficiency. Under the circumstances, students who completed five years of secondary school, and the parents and teachers of these students, opted overwhelmingly for the more clearly defined and valued general proficiency, even when a student's level of mastery of a subject might have suggested that a basic proficiency examination was a more appropriate choice. In the final analysis, stakeholders interpreted the basic proficiency simply as having less market currency than the general proficiency and gradually shied away from it.

Recognizing that the number of candidates for this examination was falling well below expectations, CXC commissioned a study to examine more carefully the challenges of the basic proficiency. An internal CXC meeting was convened on 2 February 1999 to discuss the resulting report (CXC 1999) and to find a way forward with the basic proficiency examination. The meeting concluded that "not only must more be done to differentiate between the Basic Proficiency and General Proficiency schemes, but also the relationship, if any, between the two schemes must be clarified" (ibid.).

It was evident that the response of stakeholders to the basic proficiency was less than encouraging. With the declining demand for basic proficiency, reflected in the small and declining candidate entries in the vast majority of its offerings, the offer of a basic proficiency alternative to general proficiency was gradually discontinued.

The technical proficiency fared better than the basic proficiency. According to the council, a technical proficiency syllabus and examination catered to "those candidates who require a greater practical orientation and preparation for further technical studies or pro-technician training than offered in a subject in the same area at General Proficiency" (CXC 1991, 6). Given the particular purpose of the technical proficiency, only a limited number of subjects were developed under this scheme.

In the May–June 2013 examination, only three subjects were examined under the scheme – Building Technology, Electrical and Electronic Technology, and Mechanical Engineering Technology (CXC 2013a).

The technical proficiency scheme had a more practical, job-market orientation than the general and basic proficiency ones. It had a much better response from stakeholders than the basic proficiency scheme. This might be attributed, in part, to the basic preparation it provided for certain entry-level technical jobs. However, the link between the technical proficiency scheme and opportunities for further technical study, including the Caribbean Advanced Proficiency Examination (CAPE) must also have contributed to the better response of stakeholders. Nevertheless, the subject entries remain among the lowest in the CSEC examinations at a time when there is an increasing demand in the region for technical skills among school leavers entering the work force. The number of candidate entries suggests that some reshaping of these technical proficiency subjects may be necessary to render them more responsive to the needs of stakeholders.

Post-Secondary Offerings

Once the council had firmly established the end-of-secondary-school examinations, it turned its attention to the post-secondary examinations, which were still being offered in the region by the British examinations boards. The General Certificate of Education Advanced Level (GCE A level) examinations were the dominant post-secondary offerings for those who had completed their secondary education and wished to obtain the higher matriculation qualifications for entry into certain university programmes in the region. It was evident that the continuation of the A level examinations of the British boards was incongruous with the reforms that were underway in the region to Caribbeanize all levels of the education system – that is, pre-primary, primary, secondary and tertiary. The replacement of the A level examinations was essential to the completion of the transformation of the external examination system that CXC had started when it replaced the British O level examinations.

CAPE was designed to replace the GCE A level examinations. In designing this replacement, CXC maintained the perspective that had earlier guided the development of the CSEC, of catering to a wider proportion of the population. When compared with the GCE A level examinations, therefore, CAPE catered to wider interests among students who wished to proceed to post-secondary education and training.

CAPE offerings were defined in terms of subject units, each of which would normally require a year of preparation leading to an examination. Where a subject consisted of two units, a student could, in most instances, opt to take unit 1 or unit 2 in the first year and proceed to the second unit in the next year or in a later year. The CAPE offerings allowed for both breadth and depth of study.

Students pursuing CAPE were able to select units of subjects that matched their interests and abilities. The examination provided students with wide options for selecting courses of study to upgrade their knowledge and skills for a particular vocation, or for satisfying the prerequisites for entering into university programmes. For the May–June 2013 examinations, the council offered twenty-four subjects comprising forty-six units (CXC 2013a). With the introduction of this post-secondary scheme, several schools that once offered programmes only up to the CSEC level have been providing opportunities for students to remain for one or two additional years to pursue a CAPE programme. An increasing number of private candidates are also taking CAPE subjects.

Students completing CAPE courses of study in relevant subjects and units are often eligible for course exemptions in university programmes. In an April 2010 news release, for example, CXC announced that it had signed agreements with a number of universities and colleges that provide exemptions from courses in their bachelor's degree programmes. Two of these may be cited to illustrate the nature of these exemptions.

The first is an articulation agreement with Johnson & Wales University (JWU) which has four campuses in the United States – Providence, Rhode Island; North Miami, Florida; Denver, Colorado; and Charlotte, North Carolina. The essence of the agreement was summarized as follows:

> Under the agreement, CAPE grades of IV or better are awarded transfer credit. In most cases, each Unit is awarded 4.5 credits however [sic], in some cases a Unit may attract more credits depending on the JWU course equivalent. For Accounting Unit 1, students will receive credits for Accounting 1, Business Accounting 1 and Hospitality Accounting 1. They will receive similar credits for Accounting Unit 2 at a higher level, that is, Accounting II, Business Accounting II, and Hospitality Accounting II.
>
> Known for its hospitality and business programmes, JWU offers three course exemptions for both Units of Food and Nutrition. For Food and Nutrition Unit 1, students get exempted from Introduction to Nutrition, Hotel Food and Beverage Operations and Essentials of International Food and Beverage; while for Food and Nutrition Unit 2, they are exempted from Menu Planning and Cost Control, Food and Beverage and Cost Control and one Hospitality Elective. (CXC 2010f)

The other agreement which may be cited was with St Mary's University in Halifax, Nova Scotia, Canada, which approved thirteen CAPE subjects for transfer credits. The essence of this agreement was summarized as follows: "The subjects approved so far are Accounting, Biology, Caribbean Studies, Chemistry, Communication Studies, Computer Science, Economics, Environmental Science, French, Management of Business, Physics, Pure Mathematics and Spanish. Each of the equivalent St Mary's subjects, with the exception of Environmental Science and Spanish, counts as three credit hours; those two count for six credits each" (CXC 2010f).

The two articulation agreements indicate the recognition given to CAPE as a post-secondary qualification which can accelerate the pace of completion of a bachelor's degree in a number of specializations in various universities and colleges.

An offshoot of the CAPE offerings by the council was the offer of an associate degree. The associate degree was derived from a clustering of CAPE offerings to provide a coherent programme equivalent to a two-year post-secondary course of study. The regulations governing the award of the associate degree allows for the accumulation of the required credits over a period of up to five years. The associate degree was designed for offer in nine areas – business studies, computer science, environmental science, general studies, humanities, mathematics, modern languages, natural sciences and technical studies. The award of the associate degree requires the successful completion of a minimum of seven CAPE units, over no more than five years, which must include (1) Caribbean Studies and Communication Studies (two single-unit subjects), (2) a number of specialized subjects related to the area of the award and (3) one or more optional subjects. The associate degree in mathematics, for example, requires the following:

1. Caribbean Studies (a one-unit subject);
2. Communication Studies (a one-unit subject);
3. Pure Mathematics Unit 1;
4. Pure Mathematics Unit 2;
5. Applied Mathematics (a one-unit subject);
6. Statistical Analysis (a one-unit subject);
7. One other unit chosen from the offerings in physics, computer science, information technology or chemistry. (CXC 2005b)

It was anticipated that a student who completed the associate degree would be able to obtain, in related bachelor's degree programmes offered at universities within and outside of the region, exemptions that would significantly reduce the time required for completion of the relevant programme. Although the associate degree was one of the later offerings of the council, significant progress has been achieved in obtaining levels of exemption for this certification that facilitate the seamless movement of students to bachelor's degree programmes and the consequent significant reduction in the time needed to complete a bachelor's degree.

Two examples from the CXC April 2010 news release illustrate the point. The first relates to an agreement signed with Monroe College, which has campuses in New York, United States. The agreement focused on two bachelor's degree programmes for which the college was well known – one in business administration and the other in information systems. According to the news release, "Under the agreement, Monroe College will accept up to 21 credits, the equivalent of one year's worth of credits from students who have completed a CXC Associate degree in good academic standing" (CXC 2010f).

The other agreement was with Oglethorpe University in Atlanta, Georgia, United States. It provides that "any student attaining an Associate degree from CXC will be granted 28 semester credit hours in major or minor subject areas offered at Oglethorpe University". The twenty-eight semester credits will allow for one full year of exemption at the university (CXC 2010f).

A New Offering in Secondary Level Competence

With the demise of the basic proficiency and little prospect of refurbishing it to respond to the needs of those who could not complete the CXC general proficiency within the time available at secondary school, there was an obvious need for further action by the council. The need for action was made more pressing as governments in the region adopted a policy of universal secondary education aimed at providing appropriate secondary education for everyone. A central consideration of this policy was that all students should acquire certain essential knowledge and skills that would prepare them for life after secondary school. As the regional examinations board, CXC was called upon to develop a programme and examination which would aid the achievement of the objective of universal secondary education. The CCSLC was designed as a response to this request.

The implementation of the CCSLC marked a new approach to the public examinations of the council. Whereas certificates for the other CXC offerings were conferred solely by CXC, the CCSLC was conferred jointly by CXC and the local Ministry of Education of participating countries.

In order to satisfy the requirements for the certificate, all students must satisfactorily complete a core of English, mathematics and three electives over a period of no more than five years. These electives were permitted from a wide range of subject offerings. They included the following:

1. CXC subjects developed specifically for the CCSLC programme;
2. CSEC technical and vocational education and training, and business studies subjects;
3. CSEC creative and expressive arts subjects;
4. Technical vocational education training regional Level I programmes;
5. Technical vocational education training and other programmes certified by other boards;
6. Locally developed enrichment programmes. (CXC 2007)

For the CSEC offerings mentioned in the second and third points above, a grade IV or higher was required. In other words, students would be given credit for a grade that was one grade lower than that generally accepted as a satisfactory level of attainment for a student pursuing a CSEC certification.

The CCSLC is a relatively new CXC examination. It had its first sitting in May–June 2007. It may be too early to make a proper assessment of the future of this examination. However, based on the fact that thirteen countries participated in this examination in 2010 (CXC 2010a), it is clear that the examination is viewed in a more positive light than the basic proficiency which has now been discontinued. The CCSLC concept seems to be much clearer than that of the basic proficiency. It is an examination that is cast below the level of the gold standard of secondary school achievement, the general proficiency. It may, in fact, be seen as a pre-CSEC offering, which may be used to access employment at certain levels and which may form the foundation for further education and training, including preparation for CSEC.

Within the international community, the CSEC qualification was clearly established as an end-of-secondary-school qualification and the CAPE as a post-secondary offering. CXC felt it necessary to clarify, for stakeholders, the international standing of the CCSLC. In pursuit of this objective, CXC commissioned the UK National Academic Recognition Information Centre (UK NARIC) to undertake an international benchmarking study of the CCSLC. UK NARIC is a well-known and internationally recognized agency that provides information, advice and expert opinion on academic, vocational and professional qualifications worldwide.

UK NARIC concluded its review of the CCSLC in June 2014. It concluded that "the CCSLC demands a comparable level of knowledge, skills and competencies to that broadly required for completion of Key Stage 3 (Year 9) in the UK, Year 9 in Australia, Grade 9 in Canada and Grade 9 in the USA". UK NARIC, therefore, confirmed that "individuals certified in the CCSLC demonstrate the overall knowledge, skills and competencies required to enter secondary education at Key Stage 4 (Year 10) in the UK, Year 10 in Australia, Grade 10 in Ontario and Grade 10 in the USA" (UK NARIC 2014, 82).

This UK NARIC report helps to position the CCSLC firmly as a pre-CSEC qualification. It is a good foundation for the preparation of the CSEC and other qualifications at that level.

Other Involvement in Regional Examinations

The collaboration between the council and member countries, which was demonstrated in the implementation of the CCSLC, was also evident in the provision of certification for a Caribbean vocational qualification (CVQ). The CVQ utilizes a competency-based approach to training, assessment and certification which is generally associated with such vocational qualifications. Schools which are equipped to do so offer level 1 of the CVQ in specified occupational areas. Consideration is also being given to the offer of level 2 CVQs by schools which are equipped to do so.

Level 1 qualification prepares students to enter the workforce as entry-level workers or semi-skilled workers, while level 2 prepares them for entry as skilled workers. The former is generally taken to be a secondary-level qualification, while the latter is regarded as a qualification at the immediate post-secondary level.

CXC also has some involvement at the primary school level. It has been providing examination services to Trinidad and Tobago for the Secondary Entrance Assessment and to Barbados for the Barbados Secondary School Entrance Examination. Both of these examinations are offered at the end of the primary school cycle.

In response to requests from member countries, CXC has recently initiated the Caribbean Primary Exit Examination (CPEA). This has effectively extended its formal role as an examinations board to the primary school level in the region.

The CPEA focuses on the assessment of literacies students should acquire by the end of their primary education. It is expected that the CPEA will provide the foundation for a seamless transition to secondary education and facilitate portability of end-of-primary-school qualifications across the countries of the region. It is intended to assist the region in assessing the quality of education provided in different schools and countries by using a common end-of-primary-school measure of achievement. At the time of writing, the CPEA had been piloted in four CXC member territories. The results have been very encouraging. It is anticipated that other Caribbean territories will soon use the CPEA as the end-of-primary-school assessment of student readiness for secondary education.

CXC now offers examinations and provides certification of achievement at the primary, secondary and post-secondary levels. In all its examinations, school-based assessment forms a critical component.

3 | Quality Assurance
An Important Role as a Regional Public Examinations Board

Quality Assurance in Education

An often overlooked role of the CXC is that of quality assurance in Caribbean education. Quality assurance in education has been defined variously. An adaptation from the UNESCO definition of quality assurance for higher education (Martin and Stella 2007) would suggest that it is an all-embracing term referring to an ongoing, continuous process of assessing, monitoring, guaranteeing, maintaining and improving the quality of an education system, institution or programme.

Campbell's (2010, 5) elaboration of the concept is particularly apposite for defining the quality assurance role of CXC:

> It can simply be defined as a system put in place to support performance according to standards. It implies a systematic way of establishing and maintaining quality improvement activities as an integral and sustainable part of systems or organizations. In education, this includes all activities that contribute to the design, assessment, monitoring of standards agreed upon by all stakeholders and improving quality of service delivery, client satisfaction and effective utilization of resources. It is thus a process of establishing up to threshold minimum requirement.

The work of CXC involves putting in place systems that support educational performance in the region in keeping with established standards. It has helped countries to put in place systematic ways of establishing and maintaining quality improvement to develop and sustain quality education. Indeed, CXC has assumed a regional role in education that affects the design, assessment and monitoring of standards and the improvement of the quality and effectiveness of the region's education. Much of this is accomplished through the establishment of educational standards, the training of teachers and other educators, and the utilization of assessment procedures that assure quality in education.

CXC Syllabuses as Standards for Quality Assurance

Educational standards reflect in concrete terms the mission that schools must fulfil. They provide guidance to teachers, students, parents, school administrators and other stakeholders about what should be accomplished at particular levels of the education system (Griffith 2008). Standards also help to define what performance will be accepted as evidence that the expected learning has taken place (McLeod et al. 1996).

CXC is an important standards-setting body for educational programmes in the Caribbean. Through its CSEC syllabuses, the council establishes what is expected of students who have satisfactorily completed five years of secondary education. Similarly, through its CAPE syllabuses, it establishes what is expected of students who have satisfactorily completed a one- or two-year course of study in a subject at the immediate post-secondary level. The syllabuses of the CCSLC, likewise, establish the skills and competencies that all secondary school leavers should have, irrespective of whether or not they are able to proceed to the CSEC programme within the time available at school. The CPEA programme, too, seeks to define the critical literacies students should possess at the primary school level for successful transition to secondary education. In addition, the assessment procedures set out in all syllabuses help to define what performance is accepted as evidence that the expected learning has taken place.

A CXC subject syllabus provides the student, the teacher, the school, the ministries of education of the countries served by the council, and the local, regional and international community with guidance about what a student taking the subject at the particular level is expected to know and be able to do. This information is set out variously in different syllabuses, but generally includes the rationale for offering the subject, the competencies that students should acquire and the applicable evaluation procedures. In most cases, the syllabus also provides special guidance to the teacher to help in the preparation of students for the examination.

Two critical considerations guide the development of CXC syllabuses. First, the syllabus for a subject must establish standards that are in keeping with the generally accepted international standards required of a student completing a course of study at the targeted level in the education system. Secondly, the syllabus must reflect the unique features of the subject for a student being prepared for life as a Caribbean citizen. These two critical considerations drive the CXC syllabus development process.

A Responsive Syllabus Development Process

CXC utilizes a panel of specialists from the region to develop each syllabus. The panellists must have the appropriate mix of knowledge, skills and experience for the task. Generally, the panel is headed by a convenor who is well respected for his or her teaching and research competencies in the subject. Depending on the nature of the subject and the level for which it is intended, the other members may be drawn from among practitioners in the field of study, specialists from among faculties of universities or other tertiary institutions, and persons who have been teaching the subject at the relevant level for several years and who are familiar with the standards expected of students undertaking a course of study in the subject. In developing a subject syllabus, the panel receives technical guidance from CXC curriculum development specialists and CXC measurement specialists.

Territorial spread is an important consideration in selecting members of the panel to develop a syllabus. The right complement of knowledge, skills and experience must, therefore, be found in conjunction with satisfactory territorial representation. The territorial representation is important in order to ensure that the peculiarities of the countries served by the council are taken into account in developing the syllabus. The inclusion of practitioners who are working in the field covered by the syllabus is particularly important for subjects that target the development of employable skills. These include technical and business subjects.

A syllabus may take up to two years to develop, depending on the complexity of the issues to be addressed. The process is well documented by Griffith (2002) and Stephens (2004). In her article "Formative Approaches to Constructing Syllabuses for the Caribbean Advanced Proficiency Examinations", Stephens emphasized the consultative and iterative processes involved in the development of a CXC syllabus.

The development of a syllabus normally involves an initial submission of recommendations to the Sub-Committee of the School Examinations Committee (SUBSEC) that is responsible for overseeing the syllabus development and syllabus maintenance work of the council. SUBSEC is made up of representatives of ministries of education in the region, some of whom are practising teachers, and representatives of universities of the region. The chairman of the council presides over these meetings, and the registrar, pro-registrar and heads of technical divisions of CXC participate in the deliberations. While SUBSEC is charged with the responsibility for approval of syllabuses, the critical development work is undertaken by the subject panels.

In the course of its work, the panel may collect and submit, for the consideration of SUBSEC, information on the preparedness of the institutions that plan to enter students for the examinations, and it may make recommendations about the minimum resource requirements that should be met by institutions wishing to prepare and enter students for the examinations. This information is conveyed to the participating territories through their representatives on the various committees of CXC and, more directly, to ministries of education through correspondence from the CXC secretariat. These are important measures. The panels are, therefore, essential elements of the quality assurance process.

According to Miller (2002), an important element in quality assurance systems is the consideration of feedback and opinions of stakeholders. Both feedback and opinions of stakeholders are given careful attention in the syllabus development procedures of CXC. This is one way of ensuring that the subjects and examinations offered by CXC are responsive to territorial needs. The interaction with stakeholders, including employers, teachers, students and parents, in the course of the development of a syllabus helps to ensure that a syllabus includes knowledge and skills that are essential for further education and training, or employment, as appropriate. The approach adopted by CXC is reflective of an awareness of the importance of responding to the market it was established to serve. Market value of its product is an important consideration for CXC, and this requires stakeholder endorsement of and confidence in its products. As Pond (2002, 188) puts it, "if an institution's products do not have market value the institution will not have a market".

CXC has in place procedures for syllabus maintenance that ensure the continuing relevance of each syllabus developed and implemented. The syllabus maintenance procedures include periodic reviews of syllabuses and their related examinations. In reviewing syllabuses, particular attention is given to feedback from students, teachers, specialists from other educational institutions and employers. Attention is also given to the candidate performance data for the relevant examinations. The periodic reviews lead to refinements to the syllabuses and examinations, of which stakeholders are notified. These may take the form of amendments made to certain specific requirements of the syllabus. These are circulated to institutions in the CXC participating territories.

The reviews may sometimes lead to a comprehensive revision and replacement of the syllabus, if the obtained feedback suggests that there is need for major changes. Such a comprehensive revision may be required if, for example, there are fundamental changes in the requirements of the employment sector, or in related educational programmes, that affect the relevance and validity of the course of study defined by the syllabus, or after the syllabus has been examined for a certain number of years – usually five.

Much of the data for syllabus reviews are derived from CXC's needs assessment conducted to identify areas which require attention. More recently, CXC has also instituted a beta study that follows the completion of the revision to a syllabus. This study seeks to collect additional data from stakeholders about the readiness of the revised syllabus for full implementation and to determine what additional refinements, if any, may be required before dissemination for use by teachers and students across the region.

Quality Assurance Impact at Various Educational Levels

A point worth noting is that the national curriculum of countries in the region is generally developed with due consideration to the standards for various CXC examinations. In developing their national curriculum at the lower secondary level, for example, countries in the region take into account the requirements of the CXC syllabuses. The lower secondary school curriculum may be geared towards the CCSLS as well as towards satisfying the prerequisite knowledge and skills for pursuing studies at the upper secondary level, where students prepare for the CSEC examinations.

A few years ago, one country even asserted that it "does not have a national curriculum, with the curriculum de facto being determined by each school and in practice being predominantly related to the requirements of the CXC examinations" (UNESCO 1999). More recently, Jules (2009, 16) noted that "at the secondary level, the CXC examinations have become the de facto standard". Also, Griffith and Jennings-Craig (2010, 2) noted in a recent study that "at the end of the primary level, in particular, students pursue a curriculum that is intended to help them transition to secondary school where the CXC examinations are the driving force in defining the curriculum". The standard-setting role of CXC in the Caribbean's education system, de facto or otherwise, is well established in the region.

Training Teachers and Developing Materials for Quality Assurance

Not only does CXC help to establish and maintain standards for quality education through its syllabus development and maintenance procedures, but the council also implements a programme of teacher training to ensure that the standards established for each programme and syllabus are understood, followed and maintained. It develops materials as well, to support classroom instruction.

The findings of several studies indicate that quality learning of students is associated with the opportunities available to teachers to participate in content-specific pedagogy linked to the new curriculum that they are learning to teach (Brown et al. 1995; Cohen and Hill 1997; Rickford 2001; Wiley and Yoon 1995). Once a new syllabus has been developed or a comprehensive revision of an existing syllabus undertaken, CXC organizes workshops to prepare teachers to deal with new or unfamiliar content and to use appropriate pedagogy. Workshops are also routinely held to help teachers treat with areas of difficulty in teaching a syllabus.

The training workshops are undertaken in collaboration with ministries of education. Most CXC training programmes utilize specialists with three different kinds of expertise to focus on three interrelated issues for quality assurance – namely, appropriate pedagogy, mastery of subject matter, and awareness and use of proper assessment procedures. These issues are addressed by a team that is invariably made up of persons with expertise as curriculum specialists, measurement specialists and subject-matter specialists. The council places high premium on these teacher-training workshops. They represent an important aspect of the quality assurance procedures pursued by the council.

The CXC workshops are conducted as regional or sub-regional activities that involve a number of countries or as territorial workshops responding to specific territorial concerns. Ministries of education of the CXC participating territories are expected to conduct their own territorial workshops, using teachers who were trained in the CXC workshops, thus enabling other teachers to benefit from the training provided directly by the council.

In addition, the council undertakes the development of resource materials for teachers and students with assistance from regional specialists. The resource persons to prepare these materials are drawn primarily from among members of CXC subject panels and examining committees and work under the guidance of CXC curriculum development specialists. Materials are developed primarily in areas where it may be challenging for teachers to access resources needed to teach specific areas of a syllabus or where teachers need more extensive pedagogical guidance in teaching a particular area of a syllabus. The materials are made available to schools, teachers and students without cost or at modest cost.

The signing of the memorandum of understanding between CXC and the Open Campus of the University of the West Indies in December 2009 extends the opportunities for teacher training. The agreement provides, inter alia, for a structured programme of training for teachers and other educational personnel involved with CXC examination. Training will cover areas such as useful pedagogy in preparing students for various CXC examinations and school-based assessment (CXC 2010g).

The teacher-training activities and the provision of materials are all intended to facilitate satisfactory achievement of the outcomes defined in the CXC syllabuses. They represent important quality assurance inputs by CXC in the region's education system.

The External Examinations Process and Quality Assurance

CSEC and CAPE provide a good sense of how CXC examination procedures function as quality assurance measures. There is some variation in these procedures for CCSLC and CPEA.

Miller (2002) points to the importance of external examinations in the Caribbean school system in maintaining quality in education. Through the administration of a common external examination to all candidates in the region, CXC helps to assure quality in the education provided at various levels, including primary, secondary and post-secondary.

CXC provides specimen examination papers to guide teachers and students about how various aspects of a subject will be assessed. The specimen examination papers mirror the standards as defined in the respective syllabuses.

The subject panel that is responsible for the development of the subject syllabus is also responsible for the development of specimen examination papers and mark schemes under the guidance of a CXC measurement specialist. The specimen papers and mark schemes are the prototypes used by the CXC examining committee for a subject in developing examination papers and mark schemes.

The examining committee for a CAPE and CSEC subject comprises a chief examiner and one or two assistant chief examiners drawn primarily from among specialists in the universities and other tertiary institutions of the region. They are experienced, qualified practitioners in the field covered by the subject.

The examining committee is an important quality assurance mechanism. Under the guidance of a CXC measurement specialist, this committee is responsible for ensuring that examination papers, across years, are developed in keeping with the specimen examination papers created by the subject panel. The examining committee is also responsible for the preparation of mark schemes, particularly for the problem-solving and essay papers it develops.

In subjects where the objective-type test forms a part of the examination, CXC undertakes the pre-testing of each item to ensure that only those items which satisfy the technical requirements of a good assessment task are retained and used in developing the relevant tests. The examining committee is responsible for ensuring that the final forms of these tests are satisfactory for the intended purpose.

Another quality assurance measure implemented by CXC is the use of moderators of examination papers. Before a CSEC or CAPE examination paper is finalized for printing, an experienced moderator familiar with the subject, appointed by CXC, scrutinizes it to ensure that it is congruent with the outcomes defined in the syllabus and that it measures these fairly and accurately. The review comments of the moderator are carefully considered and refinements made to the paper where necessary.

The examination administration and grading processes of CXC are important dimensions of the quality assurance process. All students prepare for and take the same examination papers in all centres in all territories. All of these students are subsequently graded on the same criteria. The exception, in taking the examination at the same time, may occur where there is a major unanticipated development – for example, a natural disaster – which prevents students in a particular locale from taking the examination at the specified time. In such instances, CXC may administer a parallel examination to the affected candidates at the earliest possible time.

The examining committee for a CSEC and CAPE subject is responsible for the supervision of the marking of scripts by examiners and assistant examiners. Under the guidance of the examining committee, these examiners and assistant examiners assess the work of candidates by using the marking schemes developed by the committee. Through an extensive process of standardization, the members of the examining committee first assure their own common application of the criteria developed in the mark scheme. Standardization is undertaken using samples of the scripts of candidates who actually took the subject examination. Members of the examining committee then standardize examiners, using samples of candidate scripts, and these examiners, in turn, standardize a number of assistant examiners, who work under their direct supervision during the marking exercise.

For several years, the CXC marking exercise for CSEC and CAPE has been centre-based. Marking centres were established in four territories – Barbados, Guyana, Jamaica, and Trinidad and Tobago. The examiners and assistant examiners who mark the scripts of the essay and problem-solving papers are usually specialists with at least a first degree in the subject, who have taught for at least two years at the level at which the subject is examined. These teachers are drawn from various participating territories of CXC.

At the time of writing, CXC had initiated the electronic marking of candidate scripts. This was piloted in a few subjects with the intention of extending it to other subjects over time. This is an important measure for modernizing the CXC operation. It is a welcome initiative which provides opportunities for increased quality assurance measures, improved marker reliability, improved efficiency and reduced costs over time. It is possible that electronic making will require some refinements or adjustments to the existing procedures for quality assurance in the marking of scripts.

Following a marking exercise, scores are collated and used as the basis for awarding grades to candidates. The examining committee collaborates with CXC measurement specialists in making final recommendations to the council for the award of grades to candidates, based on the established criteria for grade awards. The work of the examining committee and, indeed, the marking and grading processes followed by CXC make an important contribution to quality assurance in education throughout the region.

Before the grades for an examination are released, an independent technical advisory committee of senior education and measurement specialists undertakes a review of the marking and grading exercise as well as the recommendations for the award of grades. This technical advisory committee reports to the CXC final awards committee on the acceptability of the grade-awarding procedures and measures taken to assure the validity, reliability and fairness of the recommended award of grades for each subject in each examination. The CXC final awards committee that comprises representatives of CXC member territories then approves the grades for release to schools and students.

The examining committees for CSEC and CAPE are required to analyse areas of weakness in student performance and to prepare a report of candidates' work, which is issued by the council after the examination results are published. A report of candidates' work, which contains comments on each examination paper, is prepared for each subject. Teachers, students and school administrators may use these reports as the basis for taking appropriate corrective actions to improve student performance in the CXC examinations. This measure, too, contributes to quality assurance by assisting teachers and students to identify ways in which improvements may be made to accomplish the expected outcomes of the syllabuses, and this, in turn, assists students to acquire and demonstrate the knowledge and skills measured by the related examinations.

Other Quality Assurance Involvement

Much of the foregoing section focused on CSEC and CAPE. However, for CCSLC also, there are parallel quality assurance arrangements.

In the case of CVQs, CXC collaborates with participating countries and schools to ensure that the established procedures for assessing vocational qualifications are followed. Teachers or assessors assess students against established occupational standards. Internal verifiers, who have oversight responsibilities for the assessment within the school – for example, a head of department – provide oversight to ensure consistency, accuracy and transparency in the assessment. External verifiers, usually appointed from the industry, visit the schools at appropriate intervals to audit the assessment and internal verification process to ensure that they meet the established standards. CXC monitors all processes closely to ensure that the performance standards are maintained. Site visits form an important part of the monitoring process.

CXC's direct involvement in quality assurance services at the primary level had initially been limited to inputs in national examinations development, scoring of examinations and generation of reports that help to facilitate placement at the secondary level. This service was limited to a few countries which independently sought the assistance of the organization. However, with the establishment of the CPEA, which, at the time of writing, was being piloted in a few countries, CXC has embarked on a journey that will further enhance its quality assurance role in the region's primary education system and so consolidate its position as the region's principal quality assurance organization at the primary, secondary and immediate post-secondary levels.

4 | Innovations by CXC in the Offer of Public Examinations in the Caribbean

New Ways of Measuring Achievement

From its inception, CXC made use of a wide range of modern assessment practices. These include objective tests, free-response questions, structured questions, oral and aural examinations, practicals, projects and field studies (CXC 1995).

Extensive use was made of objective tests which were principally multiple-choice in nature. The extensive use of multiple-choice tests as an essential component of its examinations marked an important change in assessment practices for end-of-secondary-school public examinations in the Caribbean.

The use of multiple-choice items facilitated better sampling of the syllabus domain about which inferences were made. Multiple-choice tests are known to have strong psychometric qualities that allow greater confidence in the scores awarded to students than other assessment measures widely used in public examinations. The council was able to utilize the value of the multiple-choice test in assuring greater validity and reliability of its examinations.

Multiple-choice tests are not used to cover the total test space in a CXC examination. Rather, they are used to measure those objectives for which that form of testing is most appropriate. Other forms of testing, which include essay or problem-solving papers and practicals, are used to measure those objectives for which they are better suited. Achievement in a CXC subject is therefore measured by using a number of different assessment techniques. The nature of the subject and the objectives to be accomplished by the student are important considerations in determining the assessment techniques. Generally, though, a CXC examination comprises an objective (multiple-choice) test, an essay or problem-solving test and a school-based assessment component which may take a variety of forms, depending on the subject.

Assessing and Reporting Within-Subject Profiles

Since its first examination, CXC has been reporting candidate achievement on within-subject profiles in addition to the overall grade. Despite implementing a number of pilot schemes, British boards have been, at best, sceptical about the use of such within-subject profiles (Francis 1981; Morrison 1974). Understandably, the 2003 Assessment and Qualifications Alliance (AQA) publication, which reviewed *A Century of Public Examining by AQA and Its Parent Boards*, is silent on the issue of profiles. The same is true of much of the literature reviewing the evolution of British examination, as is evident in Robinson's (2007) more recent review of current processes and their evolution in awarding examination grades.

The primary concern for British boards has been the uncertainty about whether the profile dimensions on which achievement is reported are measurably different (Francis 1981; Willmott and Nuttall 1975). However, CXC has been making extensive use of profiles from the time of its first examinations. Teachers, students, employers, placement officers and other users of certificates for the secondary and immediate post-secondary examinations were quite familiar with the overall grades awarded by the overseas examinations boards which CXC had replaced. However, CXC presented the Caribbean, for the first time, with certificates which showed not only an overall grade for each subject, but also how students performed on various dimensions of the subject.

CXC's certificates for its two major examinations (CSEC and CAPE) report information on a student's overall performance as well as his or her profile of performance on various dimensions for each of the subjects taken. The performance in CCSLC is reported on a three-point scale (master, competent and developing competence). For CPEA, however, the actual score earned is reported.

Mindful of the challenges of reporting results of its examinations on various dimensions of achievement, the council has been carefully monitoring the extent of correlation between the various dimensions on which achievement is reported. Multitrait-multimethod analyses of dimension scores form an essential part of this monitoring exercise. Also, during the test development phase, assessment tasks are developed with due consideration to the dimensions they are expected to measure.

Each CSEC candidate is awarded a certificate which lists each subject for which he or she entered. It gives the performance of the candidate on each subject in terms of the overall grade attained. This is a numerical grade ranging from I, the highest level of performance, to VI, the lowest level. It gives, as well, a profile of performance for each of the subjects. This within-subject profile comprises lettered grades ranging from A, the highest level of performance, to F, the lowest, for each of the dimensions on which achievement in the subject is assessed.

The overall grades and the profile grades awarded for CSEC, with their accompanying descriptions, are as follows:

Overall CSEC grades

I. Candidate shows a *comprehensive* grasp of the key concepts, knowledge, skills and competencies required by the syllabus.
II. Candidate shows a *good* grasp of the key concepts, knowledge, skills and competencies required by the syllabus.
III. Candidate shows a *fairly good* grasp of the key concepts, knowledge, skills and competencies required by the syllabus.
IV. Candidate shows a *moderate* grasp of the key concepts, knowledge, skills and competencies required by the syllabus.
V. Candidate shows a *limited* grasp of the key concepts, knowledge, skills and competencies required by the syllabus.
VI. Candidate shows a *very limited* grasp of the key concepts, knowledge, skills and competencies required by the syllabus.

CSEC profile grades

A. Outstanding
B. Good
C. Fairly good
D. Moderate
E. Weak
F. Poor

As in the case of a CSEC subject examination, performance in each unit of CAPE is reported in terms of an overall grade attained for each unit of a subject. Instead of a six-point overall grade as in CSEC, CAPE reports overall achievement in a subject on a seven-point scale ranging from I, the highest, to VII, the lowest. For CAPE, a student's profile of achievement within each unit of a subject is also reported on a seven-point lettered grade (A to G) for each of the dimensions on which the subject is assessed rather than on a six-point scale on which the profile of achievement for CSEC subjects is reported. Thus, both the overall and profile grades for a CSEC subject are reported.

The overall grades and the profile grades awarded for CAPE, with their accompanying descriptions, are as follows:

Overall CAPE grades

I. Shows an *excellent* grasp of the principles, concepts and skills contained in the syllabus.
Applies principles, concepts and skills to problem situations and analyses, synthesizes and evaluates issues in a competent manner.
Organizes information meaningfully and communicates ideas in an effective manner.

II. Shows a *very good* grasp of the principles, concepts and skills contained in the syllabus.
Applies principles, concepts and skills to problem situations and analyses, synthesizes and evaluates issues in a competent manner.
Organizes information meaningfully and communicates ideas in an effective manner.

III. Shows a *good* grasp of the principles, concepts and skills contained in the syllabus.
Applies principles, concepts and skills to problem situations and analyses, synthesizes and evaluates issues in a competent manner.
Organizes information meaningfully and communicates ideas in an effective manner.

IV. Shows a *satisfactory* grasp of the principles, concepts and skills contained in the syllabus.
Applies principles, concepts and skills to problem situations and analyses, synthesizes and evaluates issues in a competent manner.
Organizes information meaningfully and communicates ideas in an effective manner.

V. Shows an *acceptable* grasp of the principles, concepts and skills contained in the syllabus.
Applies principles, concepts and skills to problem situations and analyses, synthesizes and evaluates issues in a competent manner.
Organizes information meaningfully and communicates ideas in an effective manner.

VI. Shows a *limited* grasp of the principles, concepts and skills contained in the syllabus.
Shows basic weaknesses in the application of principles, concepts and skills and in analysing or evaluating issues.
Shows basic weaknesses in the organizing and communicating of information.

VII. Shows a *very limited* grasp of the principles, concepts and skills contained in the syllabus.
Shows little or no skills in the application of principles, concepts and skills and in analysing or evaluating issues.
Shows poor skills in the organizing and communicating of information.

CAPE profile grades

A. Excellent
B. Very good
C. Good
D. Satisfactory
E. Acceptable
F. Limited
G. Very limited

The profile dimensions on which achievement is reported for a subject are based on the views of the CXC subject panel on how best achievement in the particular subject may be defined, measured and reported. In the case of CSEC subjects, the subject panels defined achievement largely in terms of cognitive and psychomotor skills. In one group of subjects, achievement was defined in terms of cognitive skills only. These cognitive skills were, invariably, derivations from or variants of Bloom's taxonomy in the cognitive domain (Bloom et al. 1956). Examples of these subjects include:

- Caribbean History (knowledge, use of knowledge and enquiry/communication);
- Mathematics (knowledge, comprehension and reasoning);
- Office Administration (knowledge and comprehension, and application);
- Principles of Accounts (knowledge, application and interpretation).

However, for a second group of subjects, the panels defined achievement in terms of both cognitive and psychomotor skills. Examples of these subjects include:

- Building Technology (knowledge, application and practical ability);
- Electronic Document Preparation and Management (accuracy, speed, and presentation and use of technology);
- Geography (practical skills, knowledge and comprehension, and use of knowledge);
- Music (listening and appreciating, performing, and composing).

For a third group of subjects, subject panels defined achievement in terms of content areas. Examples of these subjects include:

- Agricultural Science (the business of farming, crop production and animal production);
- English B (drama, poetry and prose);
- Principles of Business (organizational principles, production, marketing and finance, and the business environment);
- Visual Arts (theory, productivity tools, and problem solving and programming).

The number of profile dimensions which CSEC subject panels used to define achievement ranged from two, as in Office Administration (knowledge and comprehension, and application), to four, as in Spanish (listening, reading, speaking and writing).

Whereas CXC subject panels defined profile dimensions variously for the different CSEC subjects, that was not the case for CAPE subjects. The council took the decision to define and report achievement, in all CAPE units of the various subjects, in terms of the content of the three modules that comprise a unit. For each unit of a subject, therefore, the profile of achievement comprises three grades, one for each of its three modules. Reporting by modules makes it easier to assess the articulation between CAPE syllabuses and other programmes or courses at the tertiary level. A CAPE unit may be comparable to one or more courses offered at a tertiary institution, including a university or college, and may therefore allow a student to be eligible for exemption from those courses. The added advantage of using modules is that it permits consideration of exemptions based on modules within a unit or across units. In the latter instance, modules from different units may be combined to qualify a student for exemption from one or more courses, depending on the nature of the course or courses and the coverage of the modules of the units.

Within-subject profiles as used by CXC have significant advantages and benefits for various stakeholders, compared with the traditional approach, which reports a candidate's achievement on one overall grade only. Profiles provide more information about a candidate's achievement than a single overall grade. The use of profiles, therefore, has greater potential for aiding decision-making by prospective employers, placement officers and other users of the candidate's examination results. It enables making distinctions between two candidates with the same overall level of achievement but with profiles that show a difference in their areas of strength. Thus, a candidate can be more easily and appropriately selected for an opportunity, based on the extent to which his or her profile matches the requirements, compared with those of other candidates. Profile reporting therefore provides information that aids better decision-making.

Profile reporting provides valuable feedback to schools. By reporting information which conveys the relative areas of strength and weakness of candidates, profiles assist teachers in monitoring student achievement as well as their own teaching (Macintosh and Hale 1976). A review of the profile data of students who took the CXC examinations in a particular sitting can help teachers to identify areas which require more attention in order to help in improving the performance of their students in succeeding sittings.

Profiles also provide important feedback to candidates. For candidates wishing to re-sit an examination, profile grades provide useful information about the areas in which they need to improve and on which they need to focus attention as they prepare for the re-sit. Even if candidates do not wish to re-sit, profile dimension grades will furnish them with useful information about the areas in which they are strong and those in which they have limitations. This can help in their decision-making about areas for further study or employment.

Despite these advantages, a few concerns have been raised about profile reporting. As noted earlier, one of the principal concerns relates to the reliability of profile scores (Willmott and Nuttall 1975). In order to improve the reliability of profile scores, steps must be taken to ensure the reliability of the subtests measuring achievement in each of the dimensions. Measures of the same dimensions must also be more highly correlated than measures of different dimensions. For example, the multiple-choice measure of the profile dimension "comprehension" for a subject must be more highly correlated with the essay measure of the same dimension in that subject than with the "reasoning" dimension of the subject measured either by multiple-choice or essay. This will help in assuring validity of the dimensions on which achievement is measured and reported.

These are some of the challenges to which CXC has to respond in profile reporting. The use of the multitrait-multimethod matrix recommended by Campbell and Fiske (1959) to analyse examination data has provided CXC with a very helpful way of monitoring not only the reliability of subtest scores but their validity as well and of making any necessary adjustments in the construction of the examinations and the reporting of performance.

The use of within-subject profiles by CXC from its first examinations in 1979 is one of the significant departures from other examinations, at the same level, previously offered in the Caribbean. Considerations of within-subject profiles help to determine the content and structure of a syllabus. Such considerations are also important in determining relative weighting given to subject matter and related objectives during the syllabus development exercise. Considerations of within-subject profiles also determine the nature of the items and questions, and other examination tasks, that are used to measure achievement in a subject. Considerations of within-subject profiles, therefore, permeate every aspect of CXC's major examinations. The reporting of a student's profile of achievement in a subject is a most important contribution of CXC to secondary and post-secondary examinations in the Caribbean.

School-Based Assessment

Assessment is a broad term that encompasses the entire process of collecting, synthesizing and interpreting information, whether formal or informal, numerical or textual. It is a process by which information is gathered in relation to some defined objective and is, therefore, undertaken to determine whether, or to what extent, the objective has been achieved. School-based assessment is an assessment that is undertaken at, and by, the school.

School-based assessment in public examinations has certain characteristics. These include the following:

- *The student's teacher sets the assessment task in keeping with specifications provided by the examinations board.* Although there are instances where the task may be actually defined by the examinations board, this is not the dominant practice. The teacher is invariably provided with the opportunity to help in defining the assessment task, taking into account the environment in which the school and students are located.
- *Each student's performance is assessed by his or her teacher.* The teacher is central to the assessment, although the school or the examinations board may require inputs from persons other than the teacher in making the final assessment of the work of the student.
- *The scores awarded by the teacher are moderated by the examinations board.* Various forms of moderation may be used by different examinations boards. These procedures aim to assure reliability of the marks from the school-based assessment tasks.
- *The scores contribute to the final score of the student in the examination.* Achievement scores from school-based assessment are not normally reported separately, but are added to the scores from the other parts of the examination to provide the final scores and grades awarded to students.

CXC examinations make extensive use of school-based assessment. This use of school-based assessment has introduced into Caribbean public examinations a mode of assessment that was the exception rather than the rule. The use of school-based assessment is a well-established feature of public examinations in many countries, including Australia, New Zealand, Canada and several countries in Africa and Asia. The history of school-based assessment in British public examinations boards dates back to more than half a century ago. In 1963, a number of British examinations boards initiated the offer of 100 per cent coursework for the GCE English O level examination and subsequently extended this offer to a few other O level examinations. It should be noted, also, that with the introduction of the CSE by British boards (discussed in chapter 2), provision was made for a special "Mode 3" examination which permitted a single school or group of schools to develop a syllabus and conduct the related assessment (AQA 2003). These early initiatives of 100 per cent school-based assessment differed from the school-based assessment of CXC examinations, which utilized this assessment component, from the inception of the council, as part of the overall assessment of performance in its various subject examinations.

It was not until the 1990s, well after a decade of CXC's introduction of school-based assessment as an important component of its examinations, that the British boards followed suit. Reforms in the British examination system in the early 1990s led to the introduction of a school-based assessment component for 20 per cent of the overall marks for most subjects at the General Certificate of Secondary Education (GCSE) (AQA 2003). The GCSE resulted from a merger of the GCE O levels and the CSE.

There is evident disenchantment in Britain, currently, with school-based assessment. It is expected that, from 2015, new GCSEs will be introduced in schools for their first examinations in 2017. An important feature of these new GCSEs is that subjects will be assessed by external examinations only, except where non-examination (internal) assessment is the only way to provide valid assessment of the skills required (OCR n.d.; ofqual 2013). It is unlikely that CXC will follow the British boards in removing school-based assessment as a critical component of its examinations, given how fundamental it has been to those examinations – long before the United Kingdom had embraced it as a critical component to be included in its secondary school examinations.

School-based assessment is a critical component in all but a few CXC examinations. The exceptions are CSEC Mathematics, English, and Human and Social Biology. At the time of writing, CXC was actively considering the inclusion of school-based assessment in these subjects.

All CAPE subjects have a school-based assessment component. The same is true for all CCSLC subjects. School-based assessment is an inherent feature of the CVQ certification provided by CXC, given the way in which competency-based teaching for and assessment of CVQs are undertaken in each school. The most recent addition to the CXC suite of examinations, the CPEA, also includes a significant component of school-based assessment.

It should be noted that CXC uses the term school-based assessment in relation to its CSEC syllabuses and examinations. In the case of its CAPE syllabuses and examinations, it uses the term *internal assessment,* while in the CCSLC syllabuses and examinations, it uses the term *teacher assessment.* For CPEA, the term *internal assessment* is used. The use of the various terms might well be intended to convey slight differentiation in emphases. However, more recently, CXC has been attempting to extend the use of the term *school-based assessment*. For the purpose of the discussion in this book, the term *school-based assessment* is used in a generic way to refer to all assessments that are undertaken for CXC examinations at, or by, the school. It is, essentially, teacher-led assessment of the work of CXC candidates.

In both CSEC and CAPE subjects, school-based assessment may account for between 20 and 40 per cent of the overall marks in an examination (CXC 1995), depending on the nature of the subject. Generally, the weighting for internal assessment is greater for the more practical or technical subjects, such as Art and Design, and Information Technology, compared with the other subjects. For CCSLC, internal assessment generally accounts for 50 per cent of the marks. For CPEA, 40 per cent of the overall marks are awarded through school-based assessment. Assessment in the CVQs is, essentially, school based.

Many educational specialists acknowledge the value of school-based assessment. Grima (2003, 2), for example, makes the point that "the traditional system of assessment no longer satisfies the educational and social needs of the third millennium. In the past few decades, many countries have made profound reforms in their assessment systems. Several educational systems have in turn introduced school-based assessment as part of or instead of external assessment in their certification."

The Caribbean Examinations Council is therefore not alone in placing such strong emphasis on school-based assessment. Nevertheless, the extensive use of school-based assessment may still be regarded as the flagship innovation by CXC in the examinations system of the Caribbean.

It is difficult to engage in a discussion on the examinations of the council without having to consider the integral role of school-based assessment in these examinations. This form of assessment is deeply embedded in the examinations of the council. This has been so since the inception of the council. It was intended to give teachers a greater involvement in the assessment of their students for certification provided by a public examinations board. However, several issues have been raised about the use of this form of assessment. CXC had undertaken significant public education over the years to respond to these issues and to help stakeholders across the region develop a better understanding and appreciation of the benefits that this type of assessment brings to the education system in general and to the assessment of students in particular.

Nevertheless, there are still lingering stakeholder concerns about school-based assessment. This is largely due to the lack of a full and proper understanding among stakeholders about the nature of this form of assessment. To some extent, it is due to the way that school-based assessment is practised in some schools. This often reflects the lack of a comprehensive grasp of the concept and the procedural requirements. In the next chapters of this book, some of the critical issues surrounding school-based assessment will be examined and an effort made to convey more fully what is intended in this form of assessment. An effort will be made, as well, to explain how school-based assessment may be implemented to ensure that the full benefits are derived from this most important CXC innovation in public examinations in the region.

2 | Key Issues

5 | Individualizing a Part of the Curriculum through School-Based Assessment

The Theoretical Foundations

One of the benefits of school-based assessment is that it provides the opportunity to individualize a part of the curriculum. The literature about individualizing the curriculum treats extensively with measures to assist young children with learning challenges and with the use of technology in teaching. This literature provides a sound conceptual and theoretical base to ground a discussion on the individualization of a part of the curriculum through school-based assessment. The literature also helps to clarify instructional approaches that support acquisition of the benefits of individualizing a part of the curriculum as an important feature of school-based assessment.

Bolvin (1991, 189) identifies the following four characteristics that are common to most individualized programmes: "(a) they can be adaptive to the abilities, interests, background and needs of the student; (b) they can provide optional means for different students to achieve the same goals; (c) they can provide the opportunity for different students to pursue different goals and to differing degrees of attainment; and (d) the goals to be attained by students are individually planned".

Bolvin's four characteristics aptly define the opportunities provided through school-based assessment to individualize a part of the curriculum. School-based assessment can allow a part of the curriculum to be adaptive to the abilities, interests, backgrounds and needs of the student; it can provide various options through which the individual student may achieve the same goals; it can provide the opportunity for different students in different schools or communities to pursue different goals. In addition, school-based assessment, like other components of an examination, is premised on the understanding that different students will achieve the same goals to different degrees. Finally, in school-based assessment, the goals or target outcomes for each student can be planned individually.

Individual instruction is central to the individualization of any part of a curriculum. According to Blake and McPherson (1975, 10), "individual instruction means that the learning programme for each curriculum area is organized in such a manner as to allow each child to move at his or her own pace under the guidance of his teacher. Instruction is non-graded, enabling each child to go as far in each subject as his ability permits. Careful records are kept on each child's progress."

The explanation by Blake and McPherson captures the essence of what is expected in providing individual instruction for individualizing a part of the curriculum through school-based assessment. The instruction to students must be organized in a manner that takes into account the pace at which each student is able to progress. Also, no grading of the work of the student is expected during the instructional phase. Rather, the teacher is expected to assess the progress of the student and provide guidance that will help him or her to advance towards achieving the expected outcome. Even with the best individual instruction, not all students are likely to demonstrate the same level of accomplishment. Individual differences among students are likely to be factors affecting their progress. The objective of the individualized instruction, therefore, is to help each child to go as far as possible in achieving the desired outcomes within the time available.

Individualized instruction is clearly student-centred instruction which makes extensive use of assessment for learning. In an earlier discussion of an operational model for individualization of the curriculum, Glaser (1969) identified six elements. These are helpful in the further elaboration of the concept of individualized instruction. The elements may be summarized as follows:

1. The outcomes and sub-goals of learning must be specified in terms of observable learner performance.
2. Detailed diagnosis must be made of the initial state of the learner entering a particular instructional situation.
3. Educational alternatives must be provided which are adaptive to the classifications resulting from the initial student-ability profiles.
4. As a student learns, his or her performance must be monitored and continually assessed at longer or shorter intervals appropriate to what is being taught.
5. Instruction and learning must proceed in interrelated fashion, tracking the performance and decisions of all students.

6. The instructional system must collect information in order to improve itself, and inherent in the system's design is the capability for doing so.

These six elements of Glaser's operational model for individualizing the curriculum are helpful in elaborating on the nature of individualized instruction in school-based assessment. The value of each of these elements in providing a deeper understanding of the ways in which school-based assessment aids the individualization of the curriculum is worth considering:

1. *The outcomes of the learning experience provided by the school-based assessment task must be clearly specified in terms of observable student performance.* The teacher must specify what knowledge and skills students should acquire and demonstrate in the school-based assessment task. These may already be stated in the subject syllabus of the public examinations board. However, an elaboration may be required by the teacher, based on an evaluation of the context in which the school-based assessment will take place. Context includes a consideration of the socio-economic circumstances of the students, their cultural background, the community from which they come, the community in which the school is located and the nature and quality of the school environment, including resource availability (Stufflebeam 1983).
2. *A detailed diagnosis must be made of the initial state of each student who is required to undertake the school-based assessment task.* Teachers should take into account the level of competence in the subject matter as well as the values and attitudes that each student brings to the classroom. These are factors which may impact on and affect the student's approach to the school-based assessment task and the pace at which he or she may be able to proceed. At minimum, some form of initial or diagnostic assessment, however rudimentary, about the student's prerequisite knowledge and skills for engaging in the school-based assessment task and the student's perspective about the task would be required. This would help to determine the strengths and limitations of each student in relation to the school-based assessment task to be undertaken and help the teacher to tailor the guidance to the students accordingly.
3. *Alternatives which are adaptive to the student profiles developed as a result of item 2 above must be considered, for providing guidance to students.* This approach acknowledges that there is no one cap that fits all. Each student must be provided with guidance which takes into account his or her profile based on the assessment undertaken above. The guidelines of the public examination may permit some degree of flexibility in defining the school-based assessment task. Where this is so, the teacher may work

collaboratively with each student, or group of students, to design tasks that take into account their respective competencies, values and attitudes. Whether or not this flexibility exists, the teacher will need to tailor the guidance provided to each student by taking into account the student's profile. Thus, both the content of the guidance provided by the teacher and the approach used by the teacher in communicating the guidance would benefit from this understanding of the profile of the student. Both content and approach may vary, depending on the assessed profile of the student in relation to the school-based assessment task.

4. *As a student undertakes the school-based assessment task, his or her performance must be monitored and continually assessed at longer or shorter intervals appropriate to the nature of the task and his or her profile.* This requires continuous assessment of student progress. The frequency of such assessment may be based on the nature of the task. In the chemistry or physics laboratories, for example, where students are required to undertake specified tasks, the assessment may be undertaken every few minutes over the period of each laboratory exercise. In a field research project which is undertaken over a period of several months, in history or sociology, for example, assessment may be undertaken on a weekly basis to gather information on the progress of the student.

5. *Instruction and learning must proceed in interrelated fashion, tracking the progress and performance of all students.* In the case of school-based assessment, formative assessment is an integral part of teacher instruction. This is more fully discussed in chapter 7 of this book. Suffice it to say at this point that the results of the assessment of a student's progress should be used to provide feedback to the student to help in improving his or her learning. That should, in turn, help to improve the quality of the school-based assessment task which a student completes.

6. *The assessment information must be used to improve teacher instruction.* This feedback obtained from the continuous assessment of a student's progress should be used by the teacher to make an assessment of the effectiveness of the instructional guidance provided to student. The feedback obtained may, for example, suggest that the student was not able to grasp earlier guidance provided and that another approach may be required. It might well be that it is not merely the content of the guidance which needs to be revisited but perhaps also the way that the guidance was communicated. The provision of an illustration, rather than polemics, may be more helpful to some students. Also, an opportunity for face-to-face discussion may be more helpful to some students than written guidance or comments.

The literature on individualizing the curriculum provides useful insights into the need for, and value of, individualized instruction in school-based assessment. As the foregoing discussion shows, the six elements of individualized instruction identified by Glaser (1969) provide a particularly helpful framework for clarifying the concept of individualized instruction in school-based assessment.

The Centrality of the Focus on the Individual

School-based assessment requires that the focus be placed on the individual student. While there are times when it will be necessary for the teacher to provide general guidance to the class as a whole, proper guidance for school-based assessment requires that individual attention be given to students.

In order to optimize the value of the guidance provided, the teacher must be conversant with the nature of the task each student is pursuing, and must follow the student's progress in undertaking and completing the task. As noted earlier, the student's strengths and limitations must be taken into account in providing the guidance to improve the competencies required to complete the task and to optimize learning and achievement within the time available.

As part of the guidance, the teacher needs to ensure that the student is able to access the resources required to undertake the task. The equipment and supplies required for the laboratory tasks, for example, must be accessible to the student. The site to be studied by a student of history or the enterprise to be assessed by a business student must also be accessible to him or her, which the teacher must ensure.

In many instances, special arrangements may have to be worked out to ensure that the relevant equipment and supplies, materials and sites or operations are accessible to allow each student to complete the task. Careful planning to facilitate access to the resources required by the individual student is therefore essential.

The teacher must demonstrate an ongoing interest in the progress of the student. It is important that the teacher make periodic inquiries of the student about how well he or she is progressing. The teacher should not have an interest merely in the assessment of the final product. School-based assessment requires ongoing assessment of the process by the teacher so as to provide relevant feedback to guide student improvement.

The weaker student will, evidently, require more attention. The teacher should be able to identify students who are experiencing difficulties with the school-based assessment task and seek to help them to cross whatever hurdles challenge their progress. In recognition of the fact that students have different learning styles, the teacher should seek to ascertain the type of instruction that will be best suited to each student in the course of undertaking the task and in crossing any hurdles that may be impeding his or her progress. Much like the prescription of medication, different ailments require different treatments.

Such individualized attention requires the assignment of manageable numbers of students to teachers. Although the literature on the impact of large class size on student learning is not conclusive, it is widely held that class sizes of over thirty (and even over twenty) are too large.

A number of studies have reported that class size does not have a significant effect on student achievement (Chingos 2010; Hoxby 2000). However, several studies have reported better achievement with smaller class sizes compared with larger ones (Ehrenberg et al. 2001; Mitchell and Mitchell 1999; Nye 2000).

Meta-analyses of the studies on class size have helped by identifying a number of specific factors that account for achievement which may, in fact, be affected by class size. Among these are the amount and quality of instruction that the teacher can provide to each student in smaller groups compared with larger groups (Blatchford 2009; Rice 1999). In this regard, it is worth noting the following conclusion by Blatchford (2009) based on his meta-analysis: "perhaps the most consistent finding is that class size affects individualisation of teaching. The smaller the class the more likelihood there is that a teacher will spend more time with individual pupils. . . . Qualitative studies suggest that in smaller classes it can be easier for teachers to spot problems and give feedback, identify specific needs and gear teaching to meet them, and set individual targets for pupils."

It is evident that large class sizes affect the capacity of teachers to provide quality feedback to students. Large classes will undermine the fundamental requirement of individualized attention for school-based assessment. The number of students assigned to a teacher should therefore be carefully considered.

However, it appears that this matter of class size does not get the attention it deserves in the implementation of school-based assessment. Teachers involved in school-based assessment often complain about the challenge they face of having large class sizes and how this impedes their capacity to provide the magnitude and quality of individual guidance expected of them. Discussions which the author has had with successive cohorts of graduate students who are involved in the preparation of students for various examinations offered by the CXC confirm this concern. These discussions also suggest that one reason for some of the undesirable practices in school-based assessment is the challenge that teachers with large class sizes face in following instructional practices that are recommended or required by the council. Ministries of education and school administrators will be well advised to give proper attention to this matter of class size for teachers who must guide the school-based assessment assignments of students taking a public examination. Some of the malpractices might well have their genesis in unmanageable class sizes.

Teachers should be allocated students in numbers that will allow for the individual guidance that must be provided to students undertaking school-based assessment. Large classes which preclude the prospect of the necessary guidance should be reduced. Alternatively, teachers with large classes should be provided with the support of teaching assistants who assume responsibility for certain classroom activities that will provide the class teacher with more time to make the type and quality of inputs needed for the individualized student attention that is required for school-based assessment.

In addition, teachers need to be trained in the effective and efficient management of school-based assessment. While examination boards such as CXC may provide some training for teachers, ministries of education should make an investment in the training needed by teachers to improve their understanding of the requirements of school-based assessment and their proficiency in providing individual guidance to students for this component of the examination.

The CXC Guidelines

The requirements and expectations of CXC for its school-based assessment are in keeping with the theoretical foundations of the individualized curriculum and its related instructional requirements. This was evident in the foregoing discussion. An elaboration of some aspects of the discussion would be helpful in illustrating further how CXC, as a public examinations board, operationalizes various elements of the theoretical foundations. One aspect of this will be done in this section, while other aspects will receive attention in other chapters of this book where it is more appropriate to do so.

In the *Internal Assessment Manual for Principals*, the CXC (2010h, 1) emphasizes the point that "Internal Assessment provides many opportunities for teachers and candidates to organise the learning activities of selected sections of the curriculum to meet the individual needs of each candidate".

This requires an understanding of the individual needs of the student, which may be derived from the diagnosis discussed previously. As noted earlier, this includes an assessment of the competencies that a student brings to the classroom, which may impact on the pace at which he or she is able to proceed with the school-based assessment task. It requires, as well, an understanding of the values and attitudes that the student brings to the classroom which may impact on, and affect, his or her approach to the school-based assessment task.

Broomes (1997, 4) explains that

> over the years, CXC has encouraged the development of an assessment culture in which classroom teachers and CXC play complementary roles in assessing students' performance . . .
>
> The curriculum practices supported by CXC syllabuses view internal assessment as an integral part of the assessment model. The coursework and related activities

undertaken by CXC under the guidance of the teacher, are regarded as a principal mechanism for enriching the curriculum and developing it in ways more responsive to the needs of individual students and of the special community in which the students live and have their being.

This latitude to organize learning activities of a part of the curriculum to respond to the individual needs of the students is central to school-based assessment as defined by CXC. It ensures "a better match between what is done in individual schools by individual students and what is being examined" (Broomes 1997, 5). This is so for all examinations with a school-based assessment component.

The individualizing of a part of the curriculum is, without doubt, a most commendable provision for the proper and effective education of students. The extent to which the opportunity is provided through school-based assessment for individualizing the curriculum in public examinations may vary among subjects and among public examinations boards. CXC, in most of its subjects, provides for school-based assessment to contribute 20 per cent of the overall marks for the examination. Essentially, this provides the opportunity to individualize approximately 20 per cent of the curriculum. Exceptions to this proportion are made for subjects that are more practical or performance-oriented. Such subjects include those under the home economics cluster and those under the visual and performing arts cluster, where the percentage for school-based assessment may account for 30 to 60 per cent of the overall marks, depending on the nature of the subject.

The individualization is pursued variously as is evidenced by a review of a cross-section of CXC syllabuses. The CSEC Physics syllabus, for example, which requires students to undertake a project for 20 per cent of the marks, states that "School Based Assessment provides an opportunity to individualize a part of the curriculum to meet the needs of students. It facilitates feedback to the student at various stages of the experience. This helps to build the self-confidence of the students as they proceed with their studies" (CXC 2013e, 62).

The CAPE Management of Business syllabus, as another example, requires students to undertake a project for 20 per cent of the marks. The guidance in the syllabus clearly states that "the Project should afford students the opportunity to pursue areas of personal interest" (CXC 2013c, 41).

Also, the CXC CCSLC syllabus in Mathematics that allows 50 per cent of the marks for teacher assessment provides for an assessment task, with the latitude that "teachers may adapt the tasks to reflect local or individual interests" (CXC 2012b, 4). For the CPEA, one of the main features of the assessment model is "making the assessment process within each school participatory, dynamic and flexible" (CXC 2011, 7).

The opportunity for the teacher to work with students in selecting, defining, or undertaking assignments, taking into account their interests or capability, contributes to the individualizing of a part of the curriculum. Moreover, the student benefits from planning the assignment with the teacher and in setting attainable targets. Thus, the guidance given by the teacher to a student is individualized, taking into account the interests and capability of the student. The objective to be accomplished remains the same for all students, but the approach to achieving the same end is tailored to respond to the individual student.

Individual investigations, project work and production pieces form the basis of much of the opportunities provided by school-based assessment for individualizing a part of the curriculum in public examinations. The assignments that students are required to undertake provide the opportunity for them to explore more fully an aspect of the subject being taken, in keeping with their special interests, the environment in which they are located and other special circumstances.

Despite this opportunity for individualizing a part of the curriculum, the teacher and student are required to work within the parameters defined by the public examinations board. This is one of the considerations to which attention was already called, in discussing the relevance of Glaser's (1969) operational model for individualizing instruction. The student must work under the guidance of the teacher to undertake an activity or a set of activities within the framework and guidelines established by the public examinations board. This ensures that the work undertaken is valid for the subject and that it meets the standard associated with assessment of the particular subject.

Public examinations boards have long recognized and accepted the educational value of catering for differences in interests among students. This has been done in at least three different ways. First, a board may grant permission to a school preparing candidates for examination in a particular subject, to pursue an area of study that may be uniquely relevant to the particular school or to the community in which the school is located. At the time of writing, the History syllabus for the CXC CSEC examinations, for example, requires candidates to study a core and three of the themes defined by the syllabus. However, students may replace one of the three themes with another theme identified and developed by the school. The theme must meet certain requirements, and prior approval must be obtained from the council well in advance of the examination (CXC 2010d). This theme will then be included in the assessment of the external component of the examination.

The second way in which public examinations have catered for individual differences in interest among students is by making provisions for optional papers or optional sections that relate to different aspects of the subject. At the time of writing, paper 2 of the CXC CSEC History examination, for example, required candidates to answer questions from three of the nine themes assessed.

The third way in which public examinations have catered for individual differences in interest among students is by making provisions for optional questions in papers or sections of papers. At the time of writing, paper 2 of the CXC CSEC History examinations, for example, provided two questions on each theme that a candidate selects, from which one must be answered (CXC 2010e). The provision of optional themes or papers, sections and questions caters to the interests of individual students and provides the opportunity for individual students to optimize their achievement in the examination, based on the aspect of the syllabus in which they feel that they have developed the highest degree of competence.

It is evident that public examinations boards have long recognized and accepted the educational imperative of

1. catering for the interests, backgrounds and needs of the individual student;
2. providing various means by which the individual student may develop and demonstrate the skills defined in the curriculum;
3. allowing options for the individual student to optimize his or her achievement of the pertinent skills and competencies associated with the subject.

The opportunity that is provided by school-based assessment for individualizing a part of the curriculum is not at variance with the concept of and practice in public examinations. Rather, it provides another, and perhaps a better, opportunity for public examinations to respond to the interests of individual students.

6 | Developing and Assessing Skills Often Excluded from Conventional Public Examinations

The Inherent Challenge

The conventional public examination is administered in one or more papers on specified days for specified durations, normally between one and three hours. A public examination which is administered to eleven-plus students for the purpose of selection for, or placement in, the secondary school system may, for example, comprise a single, externally set paper for each of three or four key subjects. Each paper may allow no more than one and a half hours for completion.

Generally, CXC examinations comprise both the conventional papers and a school-based assessment component. Both the CSEC and the CPEA have an external paper (paper 1) which allows one hour and fifteen minutes for completion. Both of these examinations also carry an external or school-based assessment component (paper 2).

The typical subject examination offered by the CXC at CSEC and CAPE requires two external papers. The typical completion time for the first, paper 1, is one and a half hours, while the typical completion time for the second, paper 2, is two and a half hours. Variations may occur, depending on the nature of the subject and the level of the examination. In CXC CSEC and CAPE examinations, school-based assessment is usually the "third paper", paper 3.

The conventional public examinations have certain inherent limitations. These relate, essentially, to the inability to assess certain skills which students are expected to develop and demonstrate as a result of having completed the course of study leading to the examinations. The user of the assessment results often infers that the test scores or grades are good indicators of the level of attainment of the student in all facets of the subject for which the examination was taken. The validity of such inference is questionable if the examinations from which the scores or grades are derived fail to assess certain expected outcomes. The very nature of the external papers often precludes the proper assessment of certain critical skills defined as part of a course. School-based assessment is able to fill this gap. School-based assessment is uniquely suited to test skills that cannot be tested or cannot be easily or adequately tested in a conventional public examination.

An important objective of assessing students in a subject in a public examination is to determine and report their levels of attainment. The curriculum and the teaching strategies for each subject should allow students to develop the competencies defined for the course of study. Invariably, these are not limited to cognitive skills. It is expected that students will develop competencies in making use of these skills and in applying them to explain certain phenomena or to resolve certain issues. In today's world, these are important skills for success in further education and training, for living fulfilling lives and for making useful contributions in various forms of employment.

The typical public examination, with its papers to be completed in limited time, is generally not able to assess these competencies. These papers are limited to those competencies which can be assessed in the limited time and in the format which these examinations permit. They are, invariably, unable to utilize the mix of tasks needed to cover adequately the total domain about which inferences are to be made from the test scores.

Under the circumstances, the scores of the students cannot be relied on as valid measures of the extent to which the competencies defined for a subject or course have been accomplished. Therefore, the grades and scores issued to students would have limitations in the inferences that can be made from them about the level of competence students have achieved in the domains defined by the course.

School-based assessment provides the opportunity for the development, demonstration and assessment of these competencies. By contribution to the overall scores and grades, they enhance the validity of the inferences made from the scores about the competence of students who have taken a particular course.

Responding to the Backwash Effect of the Conventional Examination

Teachers preparing students for a public examination generally focus on what will be assessed. This is rational behaviour on the part of teachers. Indeed, parents and other stakeholders would value and support this focus. After all, they all wish to see high student performance in these public examinations. This rational behaviour on the part of teachers is often characterized, pejoratively, as teaching to the test. However, the teachers who are held accountable for demonstrating that they have prepared students well for the public examination must look to student results for vindication. Good results in public examinations are expected by everyone – the students, the parents, the school administrators, the ministries of education and the teachers themselves. The negative criticism of this obviously rational behaviour on the part of teachers in preparing students for a public examination often derives from the view, and correctly so, that the teacher often excludes from consideration valuable competencies that students are expected to acquire through the particular course of study leading to the examinations.

But teaching to the test should not be derided. Rather, the focus of the concern should be the test that excludes the assessment of critical competencies. If the test included all the required competencies, and teachers taught to the test, they would merely be seeking to fully satisfy the development of the full range of competencies associated with the course of study.

Popham (2001) sought to make the distinction between good and bad dimensions of teaching to the test. He separated what he characterized as "item-teaching" from "curriculum-teaching". Popham (2001, 16) characterized item-teaching as "instruction either around the actual items found on a test or around a set of look-alike items", while curriculum-teaching, in his view, "requires teachers to direct their instruction towards a specific body of content knowledge or a specific set of cognitive skills represented by the test". He decries the former practice. Helpful though this distinction may be in reshaping the views about teaching to the test, Popham's focus is still on cognitive skills, no doubt because of the focus of his discussion on the conventional test. In today's world, proper student preparation must transcend teaching for the development of cognitive skills. In this sense, Popham's curriculum-teaching, as defined, still has limitations that should be avoided.

Teaching to the test can only be acceptable if the test is a comprehensive measure of the competencies that students are expected to develop as a result of completing a particular course of study. If the test covers these competencies comprehensively and the teacher provides preparation in keeping with what is tested, then this cannot be regarded as unacceptable. Therein lies the challenge. Does the test really measure the competencies the student is expected to develop? If it is the typical test of a public examination, then it is unlikely to cover all these competencies. However, if school-based assessment were to be included as part of the test, the opportunities will be provided for doing so.

School-based assessment is able to assess critical competencies students are expected to develop but which cannot be easily measured, if they can be measured at all, by the conventional forms of tests associated with public examinations.

School-based assessment, therefore, has a special place in assuring the validity of teacher preparation of students and the validity of the inferences to be drawn from test scores as measures of competencies in a course of study completed by students.

School-based assessment does, in fact, facilitate an alignment between what Porter (2006) calls the intended, enacted, assessed and learned curricula. In the case of public examinations such as those offered by CXC, the intended curriculum would be the detailed syllabus developed for each subject. It provides guidance to the teacher, the student and other stakeholders about the competencies students are expected to have upon completing the course of study. The enacted curriculum would be what teachers actually cover with students in the particular subject as they prepare for the public examination. The assessed curriculum would be what is assessed in the public examination to determine the level of competence of students in a particular subject. Finally, the learned curriculum would be what was learned by students and the level of proficiency achieved.

If the assessment fails to comprehensively cover the intended curriculum, then teachers are likely to restrict their teaching to what is being assessed – that is, the assessed curriculum. They are likely to perceive the public examination as a better definition of what should be taught than the syllabus or other guidelines provided for the public examination. The enacted curriculum will, therefore, fall short of the intended curriculum. Student learning, the learned curriculum will, consequently, fall short of the intended curriculum. Essentially, therefore, if the test represents a distortion of the intended curriculum, the validity of what is taught and learned will be seriously compromised.

School-based assessment permits the assessment of those competencies which are critical to the intended curriculum but which are not easily assessed, or cannot be easily assessed, by the conventional public examination. It provides an opportunity to treat with the limitations in making inferences about student competencies from scores or grades derived from the conventional public examinations which are not able to cover the competencies students are expected to have through the completion of a course of study. It is a most important way of assisting in the alignment between the intended, enacted, learned and assessed curricula.

The Importance of Validity

The validity of the inferences made from test scores about the competence of students in the domain of interest is of paramount importance to the proper assessment of students. The opportunity provided by school-based assessment to improve validity is therefore critical to proper student assessment.

Two most frequently cited technical qualities of a good examination are validity and reliability. While the reliability of inferences drawn from test scores is very important, the validity of the inferences from those test scores is essential to good assessment. This has long been accepted among the foremost measurement specialists. Indeed, in the last two editions of *Educational Measurement* (Brenan 2006; Linn 1993), which may be regarded as the bible for measurement practitioners, the chapter that treats with the subject of validity and validation has preceded the chapter on reliability, reflecting the place of validity vis-à-vis reliability in measurement.

It is worth noting, also, that Feldt and Brennan (1993), at the end of the chapter on reliability that they contributed in the third edition of *Educational Measurement*, could not help reflecting on the pre-eminence, not of reliability, about which they were writing, but of validity. Feldt and Brennan (1993, 143), with commendable humility at the end of their seminal work on reliability, wrote thus: "The authors readily acknowledge the primacy of validity in the evaluation of the adequacy of an educational measure". And this was at the end of a chapter about the nature and importance of reliability, not validity.

While reliability is concerned with the extent of the precision of test scores (Haertel 2006) – that is, the accuracy or dependability of test scores (Berkowitz et al. 2000) – validity is concerned with the extent to which inferences based on test scores are meaningful, useful and appropriate (Messick 1993). School-based assessment makes an invaluable contribution to assuring satisfaction of these qualities of validity in a public examination.

It is clear that school-based assessment adds to validity by facilitating a more comprehensive measurement of learning outcomes and by focusing classroom instructions on the development of important skills that may otherwise be ignored. In addition, the very prospect of making use of school-based assessment provides an opportunity to include in the curriculum competences that will help to make it more fit for the purpose of preparing students for their various destinations. The curriculum is not constrained by what can be assessed in the more conventional procedures which dominate practice in public examinations. School-based assessment is, therefore, a liberating force in curriculum design. It liberates the curriculum developer to include, in a course of study, skills which reflect critical competencies, without the constraint of whether they can be measured in the typical examination.

Authentic Assessment

The conventional examination allows students to show that they have acquired certain relevant skills and knowledge in a particular subject and that they can communicate this in a manner that others can understand. It essentially provides an assessment of cognitive skills, although it must be acknowledged that, in a few subject examinations, other types of competencies are assessed. However, these are the exceptions. It is understandable, therefore, that many high-performing students in public examinations often find it difficult to transfer the knowledge they have acquired to the resolution of issues in their real-world environment.

Cognizant of these limitations, CXC, from its inception, determined that the modes of examining employed by the council should not be restricted to the traditional essay-type examinations and that alternative methods of examining students should be explored. School-based assessment emerged as a firmly entrenched component of an alternative method used by CXC in assessing students' performance.

The usefulness and advantages of school-based assessment are perhaps well crystallized in its capacity to facilitate and promote authentic assessment. Authentic assessment focuses on the application of knowledge to real-life situations and, therefore, enhances the learning and assessment process. Authentic assessment requires the student to perform, or to create or produce something, based on the requirements of the curriculum. These tasks look more like the actual activities and processes in which persons are engaged in the real world. They require students to apply what they know and to demonstrate the competencies needed for success in the real world (Griffith 2000).

Authentic assessment in school-based assessment provides the opportunity for students to make the nexus between learning and living. Wiggins (1989), in an article on *Teaching to the (Authentic) Test*, illustrates the types of authentic assessment tasks that may be facilitated through school-based assessment. Wiggins describes an assignment given to ninth-grade students who were required to complete an oral history project based on interviews and written sources and to present their findings in class. Students were asked to create three hypotheses based on their preliminary investigations and four questions they would ask to test each hypothesis. Students were evaluated, inter alia, on criteria that included whether they had investigated three hypotheses, selected appropriate sources for interviews, asked valid questions, noted important differences between "fact" and "opinion" in the answers they received, used evidence to prove the ultimate best hypothesis and effectively organized their writing and presentation to the class.

Clearly, these students were required to make use of their knowledge and skills in circumstances that were like the real-life situation. They were not just asked to show what they knew about research but to behave like a researcher. This type of assignment illustrates how school-based assessment provides a unique opportunity for developing and assessing skills that cannot be easily assessed in the typical external examination. It shows, as well, the potential for enriching the curriculum by providing for critical educational activities that school-based assessment is uniquely suited to facilitate.

School-based assessments, if administered properly, can provide students with an opportunity to develop practical skills, including research skills. It may, for example, give students an opportunity to formulate their own topics and research problems, devise strategies to gather information about the particular problems, interpret the data and find ways of possibly solving the problems they have chosen. This would be difficult to replicate in a written one- to three-hour examination.

Provision of Opportunities for Authentic Assessment

The school-based assessment requirements in many of the subjects offered by CXC provide opportunities for authentic assessment. For example, the CSEC History syllabus provides an option that requires students to undertake a history research project, where they are expected to behave like a historian. They are required to identify a suitable area of research, develop a rationale for selecting the area of research, collect historical data from a number of sources, analyse and interpret the data in relation to the research questions and prepare a report using the conventions of writing that historians use (CXC 2010e).

Also, the internal assessment component of CAPE Applied Mathematics aims to "enable students to use methods and procedures of statistical analysis to describe or explain real-life phenomena" (CXC 2010b, 55). Similarly, one of the aims of the internal assessment component of CAPE accounting is to "ensure that assessment takes place in a more authentic environment" (CXC 2012a, 37). The tasks that students are required to undertake in these two CAPE subjects involve activities and processes that are similar to those undertaken in real-life situations.

The mark scheme for the CSEC Social Studies school-based assessment well illustrates the type of skills that students are expected to develop and demonstrate through this component of the examination. Students are required to prepare a project report that includes a statement of the problem, reason for selecting the area of research, method of investigation, procedures for data collection, data analysis and interpretation, statement of findings, and recommendations based on the findings (CXC 2010e).

Such real-world research experience would not only prepare students for further education and training but also provide them with skills of collecting and using data to improve the quality of their decision-making in a variety of circumstances. It would also help them to critically examine information which they have to engage in the real world.

Another illustration is found in CSEC Principles of Business, where students are required to formulate their own business plan for a production, marketing or finance operation. They are required to provide, inter alia, a description of the type and nature of the business, how they would organize and conduct the business, and the ethical issues which may arise and how they plan to treat with them (CXC 2006). Students preparing for CSEC Principles of Business engage in the actual preparation of a business plan in the same way as it should be done by a potential investor.

The hands-on experience which this syllabus provides in developing aspects of a small business is invaluable to the development of skills that reflect real-world experience. This experience will, without doubt, conduce to the provision of an education fit for the purpose of preparing the student for their various possible destinations after school.

A similar emphasis is evident in school-based assessment tasks for CCSLC and CPEA. For CCSLC Mathematics, for example, one of the school-based assessment tasks requires students to conduct a small investigation and produce a report. The task requires students to collect and organize data, interpret data, draw conclusions, make inferences and make a presentation (CXC 2012b). Also, for CCSLC Social Studies, one of the tasks requires students to design and implement a programme aimed at producing a solution to a problem identified from any one of the following three categories: alternative sources of energy, solid waste management and living green (CXC 2012c).

In the case of the CPEA, the school-based assessment requires students to engage in "activities which help them to formulate an understanding of themselves and how the world around them emerges" (CXC 2011, 15). The project, which is an important dimension of school-based assessment in the CPEA, requires students to engage in an inquiry process where they "collect some material and then organize and present the data" (CXC 2011, 16).

Authentic assessment is therefore embedded in CXC's examinations at all levels – primary, secondary and post-secondary. The school-based assessment component of these examinations helps to ensure that students who pursue them have an opportunity to develop the full range of competencies which may be expected of persons who have completed a course of study in the respective subjects.

7 | The Centrality of Feedback

The Concept of Feedback

Wiggins (2004) describes feedback as information about how one does in light of some goal. This information can be used to make modifications, adjustments or refinements that will help in achieving the particular goal. Feedback, therefore, should be of considerable value to those who receive it. The value lies in the capacity to benefit from provided information that will allow the recipient to improve in relation to a defined goal or outcome. It requires a clear understanding of the goal or outcome itself and of the standard associated with its achievement. Without this clarity of understanding, it would be challenging to provide feedback that is helpful.

Feedback must be unequivocal and unambiguous. It must be conveyed in a manner that allows the recipient to understand whether, or to what extent, a particular goal or expected outcome is being accomplished. It must have meaning to the person expected to benefit from it. It is not enough that the person providing it is clear about what he or she intends to convey. After all, the primary purpose of the feedback is to convey information to the recipient which is meaningful to him or her. A frown from an instructor after reviewing a piece of artwork of a student may convey nothing to that student. The student may, in fact, be quite bewildered by this. However, a nod of encouragement from a dance instructor may convey to a dance student that he or she is doing well. The central point is that feedback must be meaningful to the recipient.

Teacher feedback comprising an oral or written comment such as "this needs much more work" or "this group needs to try harder" is not adequate. This is too vague to convey useful information. Such feedback would not help in conveying to the student what needs to be done in order to achieve the desired goal.

The same limitation exists in the mere award of marks or grades, unaccompanied by other information. This would not qualify as useful feedback. For feedback to be useful, students would need to be given information on the shortcomings of what they have done so far and what they need to do to improve. According to Black and Wiliam (1998, 7), "research studies have shown that if pupils are given only marks or grades, they do not benefit from the feedback on their work". The authors contend, however, that "feedback has been shown to improve learning where it gives each pupil specific guidance on strengths and weaknesses, preferably without any overall marks" (ibid.).

What, then, is good feedback? Feedback should be explicit. It should be clear enough to help a student to come to a better understanding about what must be done to achieve a particular goal or expected outcome. Consideration of the feedback by the student should facilitate the closing of the gap between the output which resulted in the feedback and the output that is expected (Nicol 2008).

Although the primary beneficiary of feedback is the recipient, one should not ignore the value of the feedback to its provider. The person providing the feedback, by that very act, comes to define more precisely the gap between what is observed and what is desired. This, in turn, helps the provider of the feedback to make a determination about the nature of the assistance that may be required by the recipient of the feedback to assist him or her to achieve the desired outcome.

Thus, the art or dance instructor, as part of the process of providing feedback to a person, is obliged to make some assessment about where the student stands in relation to the desired outcome. Further, that instructor must concurrently make some determination about just what is not proceeding as expected and what measures must be taken to help the student to proceed towards accomplishing the desired outcome. Thus, feedback by the instructor becomes, as well, feedback to the instructor.

Juwah et al. (2004) aptly summarize the principles of good feedback as follows:

- It facilitates the development of self-assessment in learning.
- It encourages teacher and peer dialogue around learning.
- It helps clarify what good performance is.
- It provides opportunities to close the gap between current and desired performance.
- It delivers high-quality information to students about their learning.
- It encourages positive motivational beliefs and self-esteem.
- It provides information to teachers that can be used to help shape their teaching.

This concept of feedback is at the centre of school-based assessment. Without it, the concept of school-based assessment would be stripped of one of its most important characteristics, and much of the benefit associated with this form of assessment as part of a public examination would be lost.

Feedback and Formative Assessment

Formative assessment is, essentially, about making use of feedback as a part of good teaching. It involves the assessment of students' progress by the teacher and the provision of feedback to help them make progress towards achieving the intended outcomes.

The feedback that is provided through formative assessment is also helpful to teachers in understanding what students have learned and the effectiveness of their own teaching. On the basis of this feedback, teachers can plan interventions to guide students to cross learning hurdles and improve in areas where they are weak (Airasian 2001; Gareis 2007; Gronlund 2006).

In addition, formative assessment and the related feedback assist students in undertaking self-assessment of their progress. Students are able to identify the areas in which they are not doing well and can therefore take steps to ensure their self-improvement (Airasian 2001; Nitko 1994).

In their widely circulated publication *Inside the Black Box*, Black and Wiliam (1998) gave considerable attention to the importance of formative assessment. From their review of a number of studies on innovations in teaching, they concluded that innovations that include the strengthening of the practice of formative assessment produced significant learning gains. They observed that the evidence from the studies indicated that improved formative assessment was particularly helpful in raising the achievement levels of low achievers.

Much formative assessment takes place in most classrooms in an informal manner. Such informal formative assessment may include reviewing homework and seatwork for errors or misconceptions; observing students as they carry out assignments; talking with students to determine whether they understand a concept; and listening to, and assessing, students' oral responses (Nitko 1994).

However, formative assessment may include more formal approaches such as a short written assignment to determine how much students have already learned about a topic in order to design and initiate further classroom instruction. Whether the assessment is informal or formal, the primary purpose of such formative assessment is to identify a student's learning challenges in a timely manner and to obtain specific feedback that will assist in improving teaching and learning (Assessment Reform Group 1999, 2002; Nitko 1994, 2001). Both formal and informal formative assessments are pertinent to the school-based assessment associated with CXC examinations. Teachers may utilize both formal and informal formative assessment procedures to obtain information that may be used to provide guidance to students in completing school-based assessment tasks.

Continuous Assessment and Formative Assessment

The terms formative assessment and continuous assessment are often used interchangeably. Continuous assessment refers to assessment tasks or activities that are spread over a period of time, usually as coursework (Griffith 2003). A school-based assessment task for a public examination may be undertaken over the duration of one or more semesters or school terms. In such instances, the teacher is expected to assess the progress of the student periodically and to provide guidance which will aid his or her progress towards a satisfactory completion of the task. Thus, school-based assessment may involve continuous assessment.

However, the continuous nature of assessment does not, by itself, make the assessment formative. Continuous assessment may be either formative or summative. Nitko (1994) explains that formative continuous assessment provides the teacher and student with information that guides learning on a day-to-day basis, whereas summative continuous assessment provides teachers, students and other stakeholders with information on how well a student has attained particular targets.

The concept of summative assessment in school-based assessment of a public examination will be addressed more extensively in chapter 8. However, the point made about the nature of summative continuous assessment should be sufficient to indicate that summative assessment is undertaken to determine a student's level of achievement at the end of a learning activity and not for the purpose of giving further instructional guidance.

Summative assessment data may be used for formative purposes. Griffith (2011b) reported on the design of a teacher assessment instrument which collected summative continuous assessment data on student-teachers at particular points in the teaching practice they were required to undertake as part of the teaching diploma programme they were pursuing at teachers' colleges. Each summative assessment exercise was intended to provide information on the accomplishment of student-teachers at particular stages of their teaching practice. However, the data obtained was also used formatively to provide feedback intended to help the student-teachers improve their teaching practice.

Some authors contend that although summative assessments may be used for formative purposes by providing feedback for improvement, formative assessments should never be used summatively (AISHE 2006). Black (2004) also cautioned that there are very serious problems in linking formative and summative practices. These sentiments are not shared by some specialists, including Harlen and James (1997).

Harlen and James argue that both purposes can be served with the same data, providing a distinction is made between the evidence and the interpretation of the evidence. It is the way the evidence is interpreted and used that makes the distinction. Harlen (2005) suggests a possible synergy of formative and summative assessment by making use of the same evidence for the two purposes. Essentially, this involves the collection of data for feedback at the time a task is completed, as well as using the same data, later, from several of these related tasks in assessing overall attainment. This was, in fact, what Griffith (2011b) reported in the study mentioned above.

Such use of the same data formatively and summatively is not unusual in school-based assessment of public examinations. A task may involve several related dimensions, each of which may be summatively assessed and the scores from the various dimensions cumulated to produce an overall score for the task. However, the performance data on each dimension may also be used to provide comprehensive feedback to the student on his or her areas of weakness and how these may be improved in subsequent dimensions of the task. Such feedback may, for example, include matters related to the use of language, levels of analysis and citation of sources. It should be easy to see how this formative-summative use of data may be applicable to a school-based assessment project which runs for more than one semester or school term and which comprises several subtasks.

Assessment *for* Learning: Beyond Formative Assessment

In recent discussions of ways of improving student achievement, particularly in the United Kingdom, the concepts of assessment *for* learning and assessment *of* learning have been given much attention (Assessment Systems for the Future 2005). These concepts are related to formative and summative assessment, respectively. Since the coining of the terms "formative" and "summative", for which Scriven (1967) was credited, there has been a gradual evolution of their meaning. This is not unexpected, given the passage of time and the effort to apply the concepts to wider educational contexts than that for which they were originally intended. The concepts were, in fact, originally intended to apply to programme evaluation and were distinguished by the purpose for which the evaluation was done, as well as the use to which the evaluation data were put. Purpose and use continued to be the features which distinguished one concept from the other across the years.

Robert Stake is credited by Scriven (1991, 169) as defining the formative-summative difference in culinary terms: "When the cook tastes the soup, that's formative evaluation; when the guest tastes it, that's summative evaluation." In the first instance, the evaluation is intended to provide feedback to improve the object of the evaluation by identifying adjustments and corrections that can be made to help in ensuring the desired outcome, while in the latter instance the evaluation is meant to provide feedback about the final outcome. The former is more concerned with the process, while the latter is more concerned with the product.

Following the first use of these twin concepts by Scriven (1967), they have been applied extensively to discussions of assessment of the curriculum, teaching, learning and educational outcomes in general (Airasian 1997; Bloom, Hastings, and Madaus 1971; Harlen 2005; Linn and Gronlund 2000; Nitko 1994; Salvia, Ysseldyke, and Bolt 2007). Since the clarification provided by Stake, formative assessment has clearly transcended the analogy of providing feedback to the taster to assess the extent to which the desired outcome is being achieved. It now includes the use of the assessment output by the very object of the evaluation to accomplish the desired change. Here, the culinary analogy of Stake loses relevance, since the soup as the object of the assessment could not itself use the data to bring about the desired change.

This application of the concept of formative assessment to student learning marked a significant development in the evolution of the concept. Hitherto, the concept applied to the use of assessment data by the cook – the teacher and other "assessors" – to help in making judgements about what should be done to the object of the evaluation. As the discussion in education evolved, it became evident that the use of formative assessment data in the classroom was not restricted to the assessor or teacher. It was equally applicable to the student. The need for a different characterization of the process became evident, and this need was effectively met by the concept of assessment *for* learning.

Assessment *for* learning has been characterized as "the process of seeking and interpreting evidence for use by learners and their teachers, to identify where the learners are in their learning, where they need to go and how best to get there" (Assessment Reform Group 2002). Note that two critical dimensions of this concept are that (1) the evidence is sought and interpreted not just for use by teachers but for use by learners as well and (2) the evidence is used not only to identify where learners are but to help in figuring out how best to get from where they are to where they need to go. This makes it clear that the teaching-learning process is a joint enterprise in which the teacher and student are actively involved in the use of assessment data to improve learning.

The concept of formative assessment as espoused by public examinations boards such as CXC encompasses much of what is now characterized as assessment *for* learning. Assessment *for* learning captures the shift that has taken place to the concept of formative assessment over the years and conveys much better what is intended when referring to formative assessment in school-based assessment.

In calling attention to the difference between the concept of assessment *for* learning and that of formative assessment, Stiggins (2002, 761) notes: "It is tempting to equate the idea of assessment *for learning* with our more common term, 'formative assessment.' But they are not the same. Assessment *for learning* is about far more than testing more frequently or providing teachers with evidence so that they can revise instruction, although these steps are part of it. In addition, we now understand that assessment *for learning* must involve students in the process."

Stiggins (2002) points out that assessment *for* learning is used not merely to check on student learning but to advance student learning. The process involves establishing with students, at the beginning of the learning process, a clear understanding of achievement expectations. It requires that students, in partnership with the teacher, monitor their progress towards achieving the expected learning outcomes. Unlike formative assessment, which is more concerned with informing the teacher about the achievement of the student, assessment *for* learning is more concerned with informing students about their own learning (Stiggins 2005).

In assessment *for* learning, unlike formative assessment, the focus is not on frequent assessment of student mastery but on the use of data to inform students about their progress and what needs to be done to make further progress. The teacher is expected to provide the required scaffolding and encouragement to help the student advance his or her learning. This pedagogical approach continually exploits the student's zone of proximal development (Vygotsky 1978) and optimizes the achievement prospects of the student.

The concept of assessment *for* learning brings greater conceptual clarity to the process of school-based assessment. Perhaps it is now time to make the shift from defining formative assessment as an important dimension of school-based assessment to defining assessment *for* learning as the critical dimension.

8 | Summative Assessment of Candidates and the Role of the Teacher

Fairness as an Issue

Any discussion of teacher involvement in public examinations is likely to lead to a spirited engagement about fairness of practices in the classroom. This is a matter which requires attention since fairness is of no lesser importance to a public examination than the critical considerations of validity and reliability. In fact, the *Standards for Educational and Psychological Testing* developed jointly by the American Educational Research Association, the American Psychological Association and the National Council on Measurement in Education (2014, 49) sees fairness as "a fundamental validity issue".

As noted earlier, while reliability refers to the degree to which a test or examination is free from errors of measurement – that is, the extent to which the results obtained are consistent across various examination circumstances – validity refers to the degree to which evidence and theory support specific interpretations and uses of test scores. In public examinations, fairness, which may be viewed as an important validity issue, is a critical consideration.

The *Standards for Educational and Psychological Testing* (AERA, APA and NCME 1999) provides an explanation of fairness that properly defines this technical quality in tests and examinations. According to the 1999 standards, fairness involves a lack of bias, equitable treatment in the testing process and equal scores for students who have equal standing on the tested constructs. The subsequent edition of *Standards for Educational and Psychological Testing* (AERA, APA and NCME 2014) defines two additional considerations. The first is accessibility, which requires that all those assessed should have "an unobstructed opportunity to demonstrate their standing on the construct(s) being measured" (p. 49). The second is universal design, which requires clarity on the part of the assessor "on the construct(s) to be measured, including the target of the assessment, the purpose for which scores will be used, the inferences that will be made from the scores, and the characteristics of the examinees and subgroups of the intended . . . population that could influence access" (p. 50). The concept of fairness in assessment is evidently wide and covers an extensive range of issues. The central considerations, however, revolve around the need to avoid bias and to provide equitable treatment in the assessment process. It is this essence of fairness which needs to be considered in implementing school-based assessment and which is the focus of the concept as used in the rest of this chapter.

Much of the value of a public examination would be eroded if the community of stakeholders considers it to be unfair. It is, perhaps, for that reason that fairness has come to be regarded as an essential element of a good public examination.

A group working on this issue of fairness, in a document developed under the aegis of the World Bank, supported the view that public examinations should be conducted in a manner that is regarded as fair (World Bank Group 2002a). They were of the view that these examinations should have a high degree of public acceptance. Additionally, they pointed out that there should be no particular candidate or group of candidates benefiting from an unfair advantage over others. Essentially, the examinations should be free from bias and should treat all candidates equitably.

Since the inception of public examinations, fairness has been regarded as a characteristic that must be preserved. In chapter 1, it was noted that there is general agreement that the Chinese were the first to use public examinations, which they instituted to measure the proficiency of candidates for public office and to reduce patronage (DuBois 1970; Rogers 1995). Over the ensuing years, as with most high-stakes examinations, there were growing concerns about how to counter avenues for compromising the fairness of these examinations. Hu (1984) explained that by the time of the Han dynasty, for example, between 206 BC and AD 220, the system had to guard against several factors that could potentially compromise the examinations, including the taking of notes into the examination, impersonation, and bribery of examiners.

Fairness is a central aspect of public examinations, and any inherent unfairness in any aspect of these examinations would be contradictory to the concept. While public examinations have gained general acceptance as valid, reliable and fair measures of student achievement, there is still much concern about the fairness or unfairness of the school-based assessment component of such examinations. Despite these concerns, school-based assessment has remained a central aspect of the public examinations offered by many boards, including CXC.

For some examination systems, school-based assessment is the only basis for the assessment of students and the award of certificates. Maxwell, in a paper presented at the Third Conference of the Association of Commonwealth Examination and Assessment Boards in 2004, shared the prevailing position in the state of Queensland in Australia, for example, which had abolished external examinations more than three decades previously and had replaced them with a system of school-based assessment (Maxwell 2004). Although reforms may result in some adjustments, it is clear that school-based assessment, so firmly entrenched in that system, will, in the foreseeable future, remain an integral part of the Queensland approach.

School-based assessment will, no doubt, continue to have a place in many examination systems. Nevertheless, the concerns of fairness, or lack of it, that stakeholders often raise about this type of assessment needs to be addressed so as to strengthen confidence in the practice.

The Dual Role of the Teacher

Public examinations boards have done much to assure fairness in school-based assessment. However, there is still some concern about practices in the classroom which leave some stakeholders feeling less than satisfied about the fairness of the scores awarded in school-based assessment. Many of these concerns revolve around the role of the teacher.

School-based assessment requires teachers to play a dual and seemingly paradoxical role in a public examination – that of both instructor and final assessor. This role of being both instructor and final assessor in the school-based assessment process often presents a dilemma for teachers themselves, in addition to creating uneasiness among other stakeholders.

The differential nature of the inputs often made to the school-based assessment assignments by teachers of different schools is a major factor contributing to the uneasiness of stakeholders. Some teachers may, in fact, unfairly reward students, while others may unfairly penalize them. At one end of the spectrum are teachers who may treat school-based assessment assignments very much like an external examination. In these circumstances, the student is required to undertake the assignment without any teacher guidance, and the role of the teacher is reduced to the mere assessment of the finished product. At the other extreme are teachers who may, unwittingly or otherwise, end up doing much of the assignment for the student by virtue of the nature and magnitude of the inputs that they provide to students. In such instances, the finished product does not reflect the level at which the student would be able to perform, should he or she be asked to undertake a similar task. The marks awarded for the finished product is, therefore, not a valid measure of the student's level of achievement.

A proper understanding of the line of demarcation between the teacher's role in guiding the student in school-based assessment and his or her role in assessing the student's achievement is needed. It is imperative that teachers and other stakeholders understand where the line should be drawn in order to make a proper determination of what is fair and valid and what is unfair and invalid. The nature and scope of inputs that the teacher is required to make in the school-based assessment process must be clear. It is equally important to be clear about the nature and timing of the final assessment that must be undertaken of the school-based assessment task. This requires an understanding of the difference between the role of the teacher in formative assessment, or more appropriately, assessment *for* learning and the role of the teacher in summative assessment or assessment *of* learning.

The Teacher's Formative Assessment Role

School-based assessment brings assessment and teaching together for the benefit of the student and provides the teacher with the opportunity to participate in a unique way in the assessment process that leads to the final grade awarded to a student (Griffith 2003). In school-based assessment, therefore, teaching and assessment are both undertaken by the school or, more precisely, by the class teacher. It has both a formative and a summative element.

Support for teachers' involvement in the assessment of their students is widespread, particularly because of the value of this involvement in improving instruction and, ultimately, student learning (Lewis 1997; Paris et al. 1991; Shepard 1995). The misinformed teacher or stakeholder may incorrectly regard teacher input in school-based assessment as unfair. But teacher input by way of guidance to students is both necessary and legitimate; it is not cheating. It is readily accepted that, for an external examination, the teacher must provide guidance to the student to ensure that there is a clear understanding of the requirements of the external examination and to assist him or her to optimize learning in preparation for such an examination. It should be similarly accepted that, for the school-based assessment component of an examination, the teacher must provide the relevant guidance to the student so as to ensure that he or she has a proper understanding of what is required and to assist him or her in achieving optimally on the school-based assessment task. For both the external component of the examination and the internal school-based assessment component, formative assessment, with the feedback it provides, is a major tool for the improvement of student learning and achievement.

Formative assessment in school-based assessment, with the feedback it provides to students, does not have any inherent unfairness. This is part of good teaching and is as applicable to the pursuit of school-based assessment tasks as it is to the preparation for the external component of a public examination.

Some teachers and schools adopt the practice of reviewing the completed school-based assessment assignment submitted by a student and returning it with suggestions for improvement. The assignment is then modified by the student and resubmitted. Often, this leads to an improved mark or grade for the assignment. Maxwell (2004, 6) cautions that "where work is refined and resubmitted on the basis of teacher feedback, it is sometimes difficult to determine the current state of the student's knowledge and skill, that is, to separate the student's input from the teacher's".

If it were intended that the first submission by the student should be used to provide feedback to assist in improving his or her proficiency, the action taken by the teacher would fall well within the boundaries of formative assessment or assessment *for* learning and could not be regarded as unfair. However, the issue of unfair practice would arise if the student were allowed an opportunity to undertake further work on the school-based assessment task after it was submitted for summative or final assessment. It would amount to unfair practice, too, if comments provided by the teacher were not designed to help in improving the proficiency of the student but merely to improve the product to justify the award of higher marks or grades.

There are, therefore, good grounds for questioning the fairness of the approach used by some teachers, of awarding marks or grades intended to be final marks for the assignment after it had been completed by the student, then permitting the student to resubmit the same assignment based on the teacher's comments, with the singular objective of improving the quality of the product for improved marks or grades. Such reassessment, and the accompanying award of the improved marks or grades, must be regarded as unfair practice on the part of the teacher. Such unfair practice on the part of the teacher is often the result of an improper understanding of where the line should be drawn between formative assessment and summative assessment.

The Teacher's Summative Assessment Role

Summative assessment has been defined as "the process by which teachers gather evidence in a planned and systematic way in order to draw inferences about their students' learning, based on their professional judgement, and to report at a particular time on their students' achievements" (Assessment Systems for the Future 2005, 8). While formative assessment provides the teacher and student with information that guides learning, summative assessment provides information that may be used to draw conclusions about how well a student has attained the learning targets. Summative assessment is concerned with students' achievement at the end of a period of instruction and becomes part of their record of achievement. It is concerned with what can be said about students' learning at a particular time.

In summative assessment, therefore, the aim is to report how far the student has reached in the learning journey. All other considerations would be extraneous.

In the words of G.S. Maxwell (2004, 4), "In reporting the progress made by the student, what is of interest is the final state of a student's knowledge and capability. It is of no consequence what the state of a student's knowledge and capability was at the beginning of the course. Nor is it particularly relevant what the state of the student's knowledge was at any point earlier than the end." Without doubt, school-based assessment gives the teacher a significant role in the assessment process that contributes to the final score or grade of a student. In its school-based assessment manual for principals, CXC outlines a number of reasons why the teacher's role is central to the assessment of students' achievement (CXC 2002b). These include the following:

1. teacher assessment provides the most appropriate measures of students' achievement of the objectives of a unit of work or of a period of instruction;
2. teacher assessment is highly relevant, since the teacher is the best judge of what has been done with the student;
3. teacher assessment allows for observation on a wide sample of student behaviour in a more natural setting than would occur in an externally assessed paper.

According to the CXC manual, the involvement of teachers in school-based assessment contributes not only information that is useful for instruction but also information that facilitates a more comprehensive assessment of student achievement.

While the usefulness of teacher assessment for the improvement of student learning is generally accepted, there is some concern about using teachers to make assessments of student achievement that will contribute to the overall score or grade awarded to a student in a public examination. According to the World Bank Group, while school-based assessment has many positive attributes, it has, in some instances, resulted in inequities. According to the group, "school based marks tend to be inflated due to the assessment process, parental pressure, and in some instances, threats" (World Bank Group 2002b, 9).

Whatever the reasons may be for doing so, any inflation of school-based assessment scores by the teacher would affect public confidence in a public examination. It would call into question the fairness of the scores or grades awarded to candidates. Such a practice would be contravening one of the important requirements of a public examination; that is, it should be conducted in a manner that ensures that no particular candidate or group of candidates has an unfair advantage over others.

The mistake is sometimes made of taking a student's learning progress into account in awarding the final score or grade for his or her school-based assessment assignment. Such ipsative assessment would not be appropriate for measuring and recording a student's achievement in a public examination. The score or grade awarded to a student should not take into account such factors as the level of effort of the student in the course of completing the assignment (Harlen and James 1997). Such considerations may lead to the award of a higher score or grade to a student who was initially very low on the competencies required of the assignment but, with teacher guidance, developed these to a satisfactory level by the time the assignment was completed. It may, on the other hand, lead to the award of a lower score or grade to a student who brought to the assignment the competencies the school-based assessment assignment was designed to develop and assess and who, therefore, had to make little effort to produce an excellent product.

It would be incorrect to award school-based assessment scores or grades based on these considerations. The assessment should be based on the extent to which students achieved the criterion performance and not on the extent to which they showed improvements in the competencies the school-based assessment assignment was designed to develop and assess. School-based assessment scores or grades in a public examination are summative. They should be concerned with a faithful representation of the level of achievement of a student at the time that the assessment was completed.

While a public examinations board such as CXC encourages the use of formative assessment in helping to optimize student learning and achievement in school-based assessment, the ultimate interest of such a board is in certifying the level of achievement of the student. The score or grade awarded for school-based assessment must be a reliable representation of a student's level of achievement. The score or grade must reflect what the student knows and can do. Scores and grades should be based purely on the level of competence achieved by the student. It should be clear that if the student were asked to undertake a similar task, without teacher guidance, he or she would be able to achieve a similar score or grade. Confidence in the score or grade awarded to a student is an important technical requirement of public examinations, including the school-based assessment component.

While formative assessment of learning is an important tool for optimizing student achievement, summative assessment of learning should provide a valid and reliable statement of the level of achievement of the student. Just as the score or grade awarded to a student for the external component of the examination should reflect the level of achievement of the student following a period of instruction and teacher guidance, so too must the score or grade awarded for school-based assessment reflect the level of achievement of the student, having benefited from the guidance and feedback provided by the teacher.

Assuring Valid, Reliable and Fair Summative Scores

Teachers need to be properly guided in conducting summative assessment of learning in school-based assessment. Because teachers are often uncertain of their summative assessment role in school-based assessment, it has been recommended that they "should be supported by pre-service courses and continuing professional development" (Assessment Systems for the Future 2005, 11).

Such training should consider the issues of fairness discussed earlier. The training should also help teachers to understand their role in treating with a number of social variables which may impact the quality of the school-based assessment assignment completed by students. Students from families of higher socio-economic standing may have an advantage of easier access to resources, including better informed and more knowledgeable parents and other members of their household or community, compared with students from a lower socio-economic location. This may help students who fall in the former group to develop and demonstrate, more easily and comprehensively, the skills which the school-based assessment seeks to develop and assess. These are issues of variation of opportunity to learn, which form part of the universal-design aspect of fairness which the teacher must be able to address (see the earlier section of this chapter, "Fairness as an Issue").

The formative assessment and feedback as essential elements of school-based assessment should help the teacher to provide guidance that will help to offset some of the disadvantages to the student from the lower socio-economic background and create a more equitable learning experience through the school-based assessment exercise. However, the teacher should not discourage the student who has better socio-economic circumstances from tapping the resources available to him or her. This may, in fact, allow the teacher the opportunity to respond to the greater need for guidance on the part of other students.

The teacher's role in school-based assessment is to optimize student learning, and this may be supported through students' access to learning resources available to them outside the school, coupled with the guidance provided by the teacher. Students should, however, be guided to avoid a type and level of input from others that may compromise the validity of their assignments. In any case, the continual engagement of the teacher with the students as the school-based assessment assignment is being done should obviate the prospect of having students benefit from unfair practices. These are issues that should form important components of the training programme to assist teachers in the proper implementation of school-based assessment.

CXC is among those public examinations boards which are cognizant of the need for such training. CXC conducts periodic workshops for the training of teachers not only in setting school-based assessment assignments but also in the assessment of such assignments in keeping with the standards of the board. These workshops may be conducted at the national, sub-regional and regional levels, utilizing the expertise of subject specialists from educational institutions in the region and the technical staff of CXC.

In addition, CXC provides extensive guidance in its syllabuses for the conduct of school-based assessment. The guidance includes not only information about what is expected in the school-based assessment component of the examination, but also how assignments should be marked. Marking schemes or scoring rubrics are provided in the syllabuses to guide teachers in awarding marks to assignments undertaken for the school-based assessment component of the examination. The use of marking schemes or scoring rubrics helps to reduce subjectivity in teacher assessment and increases scorer-reliability in school-based assessment.

Moderation of the marks awarded by teachers for school-based assessment is often cited as a means of addressing issues of equity and fairness by making adjustments, where necessary, to bring marks or grades awarded by the teacher back in line with the standards of the Public Examinations Board (Griffith 2003). The CXC moderation exercise involves the re-marking, by CXC appointed moderators, of a sample of assignments marked by the class teacher. The marks of the moderators are compared with those of the teacher and the relationship between the two sets of marks statistically established. If the results are not satisfactory, an adjustment is made to all marks awarded by the teacher to bring them in line with the CXC standard. This addresses that dimension of the issue of possible unfairness in teacher assessment that results from the teacher being either too lenient or too severe. The CXC procedure has worked well (Weekes 2013). However, it does not address inequitable practices that may arise from allowing some students to modify and resubmit their assignments after such assignments had been previously submitted for the purpose of making a summative assessment of students' accomplishments.

The CXC moderation exercise is concerned with the work submitted. Once the marks awarded by the teacher for the assignment are in keeping with the CXC standards, no adjustment would be required, and the council is not likely, without cause, to investigate the classroom practices that led to the quality of an assignment in the samples moderated.

Under the circumstances, the council depends on the teacher to follow fair and equitable practices. But this would not be possible if the teacher is not clear about the line that must be drawn between formative assessment (or assessment *for* learning) and summative assessment (or assessment *of* learning). Clearly, teachers need to be trained so that they understand what is required in school-based assessment, particularly in distinguishing between formative assessment and summative assessment.

3 | New Directions

9 | The Alternative Paper to School-Based Assessment

Context

Many public examinations boards offer their examinations to both in-school and out-of-school candidates. CXC, for example, caters for the school candidate as well as the out-of-school or private candidate, in both its CSEC and CAPE offerings. The syllabuses for both of these examinations include guidance for private candidates.

Many students have had to leave the formal school system, for various reasons, without completing their secondary education or post-secondary education. The offer of the CSEC and CAPE examinations to out-of-school or private candidates provides them with an opportunity to complete their education. Candidates are able to undertake self-study, obtain part-time tuition or pursue various forms of distance learning, and take the examinations for certification that is identical to that awarded to candidates who take the examinations while in full-time attendance at an institution. This avenue for improving their qualifications provides out-of-school candidates with the opportunity to develop, and be certified in, competencies that allow them to pursue objectives similar to those of students in full-time attendance in the formal school system. These include further, or higher, education and training; improved job prospects; improved capacity to contribute to and benefit from society; empowerment to navigate life better in a modernized environment; and a more fulfilling life, generally.

As noted in chapter 4, with a few exceptions, CXC examinations at all levels require a school-based assessment component. It was also noted that CXC was giving consideration to the inclusion of a school-based assessment component in those examinations which did not have it.

The completion of the school-based assessment component presents particular challenges for out-of-school or private candidates. School-based assessment involves the student working under the guidance of the teacher to undertake the required task. The out-of-school students seeking to improve their qualifications would be hard pressed to meet this condition. The opportunity to work with a teacher may not be practicable.

Given the importance of school-based assessment to public examinations, and the equivalence of the certification provided to both in-school and out-of-school candidates, CXC needed to include in its offerings to private candidates the assessment of competencies associated with this component of its examinations. This is being done through the offer of the alternative paper to the school-based assessment.

For a few CSEC and CAPE subjects in CXC examinations, private candidates are required to complete the school-based assessment just as candidates attending a full-time institution are. In such instances, the school-based assessment must be undertaken under the supervision of a teacher from a recognized educational institution. A recognized educational institution is "a school, college, academy or other institution of learning recognised by the Council for the purpose of registering its students for the Council's examinations" (CXC 2002a, 8). These institutions must be registered in the respective countries in keeping with the local requirements. The regulations that are applicable to a private candidate supervised by a teacher from such an institution are the same as those that govern candidates in full-time attendance at a school.

The subjects for which private candidates are required to do the school-based assessment include those that generally require more practical work – for example, CAPE Food and Nutrition, CAPE Electrical and Electronic Technology, CSEC Physical Education and CSEC Music. In its *Guidelines for Candidates Writing Examinations Offered by CXC* (CXC 2013f, 6), CXC notes that "the CAPE subjects that do not carry the Alternative Paper to SBA option are: Art and Design, Computer Studies, Electrical and Electronic Technology, Food and Nutrition, and Geometrical and Mechanical Engineering Technology. Private candidates desirous of writing these examinations must complete the SBA requirements." The guidelines may be updated to add CAPE Digital Media, which was examined for the first time in the CXC May–June 2014 sitting.

In the guidelines, CXC (2013f, 6) further points out that "the CSEC subjects that carry the Alternative Paper to SBA (for private candidates only) are: Additional Mathematics, Biology, Caribbean History, Chemistry, Economics, EDPM [Electronic Document Preparation and Management], Geography, Integrated Science SA [Single Award], Office Administration, Physics, Principles of Accounts, Principles of Business, and Social Studies". CXC has been making the alternative paper available in its examinations on a phased basis. In doing so, it takes into account the potential private candidate population for the particular examination.

The Challenge of Developing an Alternative Paper

The tasks in the alternative paper to school-based assessment must be constructed as a measure of the same competencies developed and measured by the school-based assessment component which the in-school candidate is required to complete. These competencies are, invariably, different from those measured by the external examination.

This is a challenge for any public examinations board. These tasks must be so constructed that they discriminate well between those candidates who have developed the competencies associated with the school-based assessment taken by the in-school candidates and those who have not developed those competencies. In essence, the alternative paper must demonstrate both the evidential and consequential bases of validity, as described by Messick (1993). The alternative paper must measure the intended constructs and be relevant to the purpose. Also, the inferences drawn from the use of the alternative paper must be valid, and the conceptual and theoretical underpinnings of the paper must be sound. These considerations are central to the construction of an alternative paper.

The alternative paper to school-based assessment seeks to mirror the competencies that students who take the school-based assessment are expected to develop. The alternative paper therefore provides an opportunity for the private candidate to be assessed on the same competencies that the in-school candidate is expected to develop and demonstrate through the school-based assessment.

It is important to note that both the candidate doing the school-based assessment and the one taking the alternative paper receive identical certification for the subject. A "grade I" awarded to a candidate who is a school candidate and who therefore does the school-based assessment is perceived to be no different from a "grade I" awarded to a private candidate who takes the alternative paper. The validity of the alternative paper as a measure of the competencies developed through school-based assessment must be assured. This requires the development of tasks for the alternative paper on which the performance of the private candidate is a true reflection of the extent to which he or she has acquired the competencies associated with the school-based assessment done by the school candidate.

CXC has taken certain steps aimed at ensuring that the alternative paper measures the same constructs as those developed and assessed in the school-based assessment and that the scores on the alternative paper are valid as measures of the same constructs reflected in the scores of the school-based assessment. This is well

Table 9.1. Comparison of the requirements of the SBA and those of the alternative paper

Requirements of the SBA Research Report	Requirements of the Alternative Paper
In the research reports, candidates should • state the problem researched in an appropriate question form; • give the reason(s) for selecting the area of research; • select an appropriate method of investigation; • design a simple instrument to collect data; • describe the procedures used for data collection; • present data using at least three appropriate forms; • analyse and interpret data with reference to the question asked in the first task above; • state findings; • make recommendations based on findings and suggest measures to implement one.	Questions will normally test candidates' ability to • state a problem in the form of a question; • select an appropriate method of investigation; • design a simple instrument (protocol) to collect data; • describe procedures to collect data; • present data in three forms; • explain data presented in the fifth task above; • interpret data in terms of the question asked in the first task above; • state findings; • make recommendations based on findings and the measures to implement one.

illustrated in the CSEC Social Studies syllabus (CXC 2010e), where the requirements outlined for the alternative paper clearly parallel those outlined for the school-based assessment. Also, the guidance provided to private candidates preparing for the alternative paper seeks to help them to develop the same competencies expected of the in-school candidates doing the school-based assessment.

Table 9.1 provides a comparison of the requirements for the CSEC Social Studies syllabus for the school-based assessment undertaken by school candidates and for private candidates doing the alternative paper. The table presents the information as it is found in the CXC syllabus, save for minor changes for presentational purposes. The nine competencies which are defined for the research report required for the school-based assessment of the in-school candidate are parallel to the nine competencies which are measured by the alternative paper.

The CSEC syllabuses also encourage candidates preparing for the alternative paper to undertake tasks that will help them to acquire the same competencies which the in-school candidate develops in the school-based assessment undertaken with teacher guidance. This, too, is well illustrated in the CSEC Social Studies syllabus (CXC, 2010e) as shown in table 9.2. Similar to table 9.1, table 9.2 represents

Table 9.2. Comparison of the guidance in undertaking the SBA and that in preparing for the alternative paper

SBA	Alternative Paper
Activities that may be done under the supervision of the class teacher and signed off as they are completed: • Statement of problem – explaining context – one paragraph and at least one question. • Method of investigation – questionnaire, interview schedule, observation checklist, document search. • Questionnaire construction. • Administering questionnaire, recording raw data (in class); students may work in pairs. • Analysing questionnaire data using univariate tables, bivariate tables and multivariate tables. • Interpretation of the data (in terms of the research question), identifying validity issues – size of sample, type of sample, instrument limitations and analysis limitations.	In order to enhance their performance on Paper 03/2, candidates may also wish to • select a problem to investigate and write it in question form; • select a suitable method to collect data. These may include use of questionnaires, interview schedules, observation checklists and documentary research; • write out the exact questions that you will put in a questionnaire or ask in an interview; • state ways to choose the sample. State how many persons should be in the sample, their gender, age group, area of residence or class. Explain how you will get the information from them; • state whether you will use graphs, charts, tables, maps, diagrams, photographs as well as prose to present your data; • explain the data you will show in the fifth task above; • in the light of the question asked in the first task above, state what the data mean; • write at least three statements on what you have found out from your investigation of the problem; • suggest two recommendations based on your findings and state how you would implement one.

the information as it is found in the CXC syllabus, save for minor changes for presentational purposes.

The guidance provided for the school-based assessment anticipates that the student will work under the guidance of the class teacher to prepare the various sections of the report required for that assessment. The guidance provided to the candidate for the alternative paper recommends a number of tasks that may be undertaken to enhance performance in the paper. The out-of-school candidate taking the alternative paper, therefore, is expected to prepare for this paper by undertaking the tasks that facilitate development of competencies that are identical to those of the in-school candidate undertaking the school-based assessment under the supervision of a teacher. This requirement expected of the out-of-school candidate is not dissimilar to the requirements in preparing for the other examination papers in a subject. While the in-school candidate benefits from the guidance of a teacher, the out-of-school candidate must pursue options that may be available to him or her to acquire the competencies assessed in the paper.

This may be done in a variety of ways. The candidate may, for example, seek the assistance and guidance of a tutor. Alternatively, the candidate may, by the nature of his or her employment or through family or other social connection, become involved in activities that lead to the development of the competencies needed to respond well to the alternative paper. Despite the guidance provided, the way the experience is acquired is not a consideration in assessing, through the alternative paper, the competencies associated with the school-based assessment.

It is evident that CXC has already made a number of advances in developing an alternative paper that mirrors the requirements for in-school candidates taking the school-based assessment. The retention of the alternative paper for those subjects which now have it, and its inclusion in others to extend the range of offerings to private candidates, should be encouraged.

The Restriction of the Paper to Private Candidates

The alternative paper is intended for the private candidate who is typically mature, out of school, in the work force and wishes to improve his or her qualifications to access opportunities for further study, improved job prospects and empowerment to navigate life better in a modernized environment. The candidate may have family commitments or other equally demanding commitments which only permit the pursuit of his or her studies on a part-time basis. This may be either through self-study, or with support from tutors in an evening, weekend or online programme, or through any combination of these approaches.

The provision of the alternative paper is expected to provide an alternative to what may be viewed as the preferred approach, where the candidate benefits from the guidance and feedback that is central to the school-based experience. The current expectation is that the school candidate will pursue the school-based assessment and benefit from teacher guidance. According to the regulations governing the examinations of CXC, a school candidate must enter for the school-based assessment option, generally labelled Paper 3/1 to distinguish it from the alternative paper, generally labelled Paper 3/2.

According to the *Guidelines for Candidates Writing Examinations Offered by CXC* (CXC 2013a, 9): "To be eligible to write the Alternative Paper to SBA (Paper 3/2 in CSEC or 3/2 in CAPE), the candidate must be registered at a private centre. Candidates registered at schools or other full-time educational institutions are not eligible to write the Alternative Paper."

This requirement seems to be premised on the view that the school-based assessment, with formative assessment as a critical dimension, is part of the good education that should be provided to students of secondary or post-secondary school age for whom CSEC and CAPE are offered in the formal education system.

It is worth considering, also, that although private candidates taking the alternative paper do not benefit, invariably, from the level of feedback and guidance provided to school candidates, their level of maturity often allows them to function as self-directed learners who are "responsible owners and managers of their own learning process" (Abdullah 2001). The school candidate is likely to need more guidance than these mature learners. It is understandable, therefore, that the CXC regulations require the school candidate to do the school-based assessment, while the alternative paper is provided for the private candidate.

Despite these considerations, however, there are students in full-time attendance at secondary schools in the countries served by CXC who seek to access the alternative paper. Some students have found ingenious ways around the regulations that prohibit the taking of the alternative paper by candidates who are in full-time attendance at an approved secondary school. For example, where the national country regulations do not establish an age requirement for registration as a private candidate, some students have registered for one or more subjects as private candidates, directly through the office of the CXC local registrars in their respective countries, instead of entering for these subjects through their schools. Thus, they are able to take the alternative paper.

The desire on the part of some school candidates to take the alternative paper rather than do the school-based assessment may be due to the mistaken impression that the alternative paper is a softer option when compared with the school-based assessment requirements. Based on information from schools in the countries served by CXC, it seems, also, that some teachers prefer to have their students take the alternative paper rather than themselves undertake the pedagogical and administrative work associated with the school-based assessment (Broomes 1997).

It is worth noting, though, that a review of the scores of the private candidates taking the alternative paper shows that these scores tend to be lower than the scores obtained by the school candidates doing the school-based assessment (Griffith 2011a). This may be attributed to the absence of teacher guidance and feedback from which the school candidate benefits.

These findings must be interpreted with caution. The study of performance data of the same candidates for both the school-based assessment and the alternative paper would provide more dependable results. Such a study is generally not possible with data from the CXC database, given that the school candidate must do the school-based assessment while the private candidate is offered the alternative paper.

However, some preliminary investigations have been undertaken, which shed some further light on the performance in the school-based assessment compared with that on the alternative paper. Emtage (2003), for example, undertook a useful study of student achievement on the alternative paper compared with that in school-based assessment. In this study, sixty-six students from three schools in Barbados who were in the last year of preparation for the CSEC Office Procedures examination in June 2001 were administered an alternative paper in April 2001. The data on their performance on this paper and on their performance in the school-based assessment were used to probe, inter alia, whether there was a significant difference between scores obtained on the alternative paper and scores obtained on the school-based assessment by the same candidates.

Emtage found that there was a marked disparity in performance of the same candidates on the alternative paper and their school-based assessment. The mean performance of the candidates in the sample was twenty-two on the alternative paper and thirty-three on the school-based assessment, out of a possible maximum score of fifty for both.

Noting the difficulties of administering the alternative paper to the same candidates who did the school-based assessment and the inherent limitations in using this approach to conduct a study, Griffith (2004) undertook a follow-up study using a different methodology. In his study, Griffith (2004) used a regression model generated from the scores of candidates on three papers – papers 1, 2 and 3/1 (school-based assessment) to predict the school-based assessment performance of a sample of one hundred candidates who had taken the alternative paper in the CXC May–June 2003 CSEC Principles of Accounts examinations and one hundred who had taken the alternative paper in the CXC May–June 2003 CSEC Social Studies examinations.

Griffith found that, while the mean score in the alternative paper for Principles of Accounts was nineteen, the mean predicted school-based assessment score was thirty-one. The maximum possible score in both instances was forty. For Social Studies, the mean score on the alternative paper was seventeen, while the mean predicted score for school-based assessment was twenty-five. In this case, the maximum possible score was thirty-five. For both subjects, the difference between the means was statistically significant.

The results of the study suggest that the candidates who took the alternative paper would have obtained higher scores in the school-based assessment if they had taken the latter option. This suggests that the school-based assessment option, which benefits from teacher guidance and feedback, would result in a higher level of achievement compared with the alternative paper, where private candidates are unlikely to obtain the benefit from such teacher guidance and feedback.

The findings of these two preliminary studies by Emtage (2003) and Griffith (2004) reinforce the conclusion formed from a review of student performance on alternative paper and the school-based assessment; that is, the alternative paper is not a softer option as some may believe. It might well be that, in preparing for the alternative paper, candidates have not been following the CXC guidance, including the guidance that they should undertake an assignment similar to that undertaken by the in-school candidates, so as to develop the relevant competencies. It is possible, also, that the differences in the attributes of the in-school population and the out-of-school population may account for the differences in performances. These are areas for further research.

Reflection On the Future of the Alternative Paper

In considering the future of the alternative paper, it is worth reflecting on the fact that, as part of a public examination, this paper has a number of advantages which would support its more extensive use. A few of these are as follows:

- *It facilitates increased access to completion of secondary education by providing access to examinations which require competencies developed and assessed through a school-based assessment component.* This point was already fully discussed.
- *It is more reliable than school-based assessment.* The issues of fairness and confidence in the scores awarded, which often beset the school-based assessment, do not arise with the alternative paper since it is assessed in the same way as the other external papers which comprise the examination.
- *It fits the public examinations model better than school-based assessment.* An essential principle of public examinations is that the assessment is undertaken and scored by an agent independent of the school. Unlike the alternative paper, the school-based assessment does not respond fully to this requirement, leading to considerable dissonance with the concept of a public examination.
- *It is a more economical option for schools, ministries of education and public examinations boards.* The cost which is invariably associated with the marking and moderation of school-based assessment samples, at times including the movement of delicate samples or the movement of moderators for on-site moderation of those samples, is avoided in the alternative paper (Griffith 2013).

The alternative paper to school-based assessment is a CXC innovation in public examination which needs to be preserved, further refined and expanded. It can provide a valid and reliable way of assessing critical subject examination competencies which are developed and assessed through school-based assessment. It is worth preserving and developing this important contribution of CXC to public examinations.

10 | Group Work in School-Based Assessment

The Concept of Group Work

Group work for the school-based assessment undertaken as part of a public examination is an innovation that provides relevant and invaluable learning experiences for students. Gibson, Ivancevich, and Donnelly (2006) define a group as two or more individuals interacting with each other in such a manner that the behaviour and/or performance of a member is influenced by the behaviour and/or performance of other members. Group work in school-based assessment would, therefore, involve two or more students coming together for the purpose of undertaking an assignment with the clear understanding that the behaviour and performance of the individual member of the group will impact all other members and their performance or achievement on the task.

Jacques (2001, 1–2) points out that a group is not a mere collection of people but should have most of the following qualities:

- Collective perception – the conscious recognition of the existence of the group by its constituent members.
- Needs – the recognition that a group will potentially be able to help individuals within its membership.
- Shared aims – the recognition of aims or incentives that motivate group members.
- Interdependence – the relationships between the members within a group depend on the contributions and behaviours of its constituent members.

- Social organization – there is an intrinsic order to a group which encompasses various rules and power relations.
- Interaction – the potential for communicative exchange must occur within groups even if members may not be geographically in the same place.
- Cohesiveness – members of a group should want the group to continue and have a desire to contribute to and benefit from it.
- Membership – a group can be defined by the extent of its membership relations. There must be a sense of exchange in a group – that is, "two or more people interacting for longer than a few minutes".

These qualities or characteristics may be easily discerned in a group undertaking school-based assessment tasks.

Group work may be defined as tasks carried out by learners working in small, cooperative groups (Nunan 2004). Such group work involves a structured process that requires learners to work together on a particular task and, in doing so, share information and encourage and support each other (Coppola 1996; Slavin 1986). The teacher designs the exercises, activities, experiences or problems that the learners must engage in. These are often well structured and may include objectives, time constraints and detailed formats for presentations and even evaluation guidelines for undertaking the task (Cranton 1996).

Johnson, Johnson and Smith (1991) classify cooperative groups involved in group work into three general types. These are informal cooperative learning groups, formal cooperative learning groups and cooperative base groups.

Informal learning groups involve the ad hoc or temporary assignment of students together, within a single class session. These groups are used to help focus students' attention on materials to be learned, set a mood conducive to learning, help organize in advance the material to be covered in a class session, ensure that students cognitively process the material being taught and provide closure to a class session.

Formal learning groups are teams established to complete a specific task. In these groups, students work together for one or several class sessions to achieve shared learning goals and jointly complete the specific task or assignment.

Base groups are long-term groups, usually existing over the course of a semester. The responsibility of such groups is primarily to provide members with support, encouragement and assistance in completing course requirements.

The characteristics of groups undertaking school-based assessment tasks for a public examination are more in keeping with the formal learning group. They comprise teams of two or more students established to undertake a specific task. It is expected that students in these groups will work together to achieve shared learning goals and jointly complete the specific school-based assessment task.

However, elements of the informal learning group and the base group may be present in the groups undertaking the school-based assessment task. The task may sometimes be of a long-term nature. It may spread across one or more semesters and may require support, encouragement and assistance from members of the group to ensure completion of certain aspects of the task assigned to individuals in the group. In this regard, elements of the base group may be evident. Also, during the period that the group is benefiting from the guidance of the teacher, particularly during in-class sessions, a number of the characteristics of the informal learning group may be manifested, as members of the group seek to help each other to focus attention on the guidance provided and materials to be learned in order to complete the task satisfactorily.

The Value of Group Work

When properly conducted, group work holds considerable benefits for school-based assessment. It provides peer support and encourages peer learning, which contribute to improved student achievement. Johnson and Johnson (2004) cite a number of studies that show that peers have a very powerful influence on students' achievement-oriented behaviour. According to the authors, when students work in cooperative learning groups, they become deeply involved in each other's learning. They help each other to learn. Students learn from each other by benefiting from the opportunity to clarify and refine their understanding of concepts through discussion and rehearsals. Given the obvious benefits of group work, students will form groups whether or not this is a requirement for school-based assessment or other assignments they must undertake during a course of study.

Group work supports the learner-centred approach to instruction and, particularly, the constructivist approach, which is espoused for its value in improving student learning. In this approach, students are seen as active participants in learning and as "co-constructors of knowledge" (Meece 2003, 111). Discovery, inquiry and problem-solving are central to the approach. Here, teachers assume more the role of facilitators of the learning process (Law 2007) than that of information dispensers (Jonassen, Myers and McKillop 1996). This position is supported by Alesandrini and Larson (2002), who make the point that, in a constructivist classroom, the teacher's role is not to lecture or provide structured, step-by-step guidance to students towards the mastery of some teacher-imposed goal but to function as a facilitator who coaches learners as they follow their own path towards personally meaningful goals.

Essentially, in the constructivist approach to teaching and learning, the teacher serves as a facilitator who encourages student exploration and questioning to help them generate their own ideas and conclusions and to construct new understandings and acquire new skills. Students are encouraged to learn by incorporating new information and skills into what they already know and believe and into the ideas that they bring to the classroom (Griffith 2006).

Group work in school-based assessment supports the constructivist approach, which is encouraged by many educators. It promotes the development of metacognitive and metalinguistic skills and enhances the application, analysis, synthesis and evaluation skills of the students (Cipolle, Funston and Johnson 2000). These considerations support the extensive use of group work in school-based assessment in public examinations such as those of CXC.

Group work enhances the contribution which school-based assessment can make in providing students with authentic learning experiences which prepare them to function better in the real world, including the work environment. It is widely acknowledged that group work helps to develop among students certain generic skills sought by employers or in professions. These include teamwork and leadership skills, collaborative and conflict management skills, and organizational and time management skills (Bourner, Hughes and Bourner 2001; Davies 2009; Maguire and Edmondson 2001).

Working in groups is often an essential work requirement, and recruiters will increasingly give weighting to experience that potential employees have in working in group settings which would have provided the opportunity for the development of competencies associated with employability (Bourner, Hughes and Bourner 2001; Davies 2009; Maguire and Edmondson 2001). Group work can therefore be seen as providing authentic experience for students, as they engage in and practice behaviours that are required in the real world of employment to which most will proceed (Davies 2009).

Additionally, the use of group work in school-based assessment has the advantage of freeing the teacher of the demands of providing individual guidance to each student in the class in undertaking the school-based assessment task. This way, the teacher is able to have a much deeper engagement in the subject matter with groups of students and to provide more extensive feedback to help in optimizing their learning and achievement in relation to the school-based assessment task.

Group work requiring the submission of a single group assignment will also reduce the workload of the teacher in the summative assessment of students on the school-based assessment task, since fewer pieces of work will now have to be assessed. Particularly in the case of larger classes, such group assignments will considerably reduce the workload for teachers. Properly handled, it can also reduce the workload of students, thus adding another benefit to those already mentioned.

Setting Up Group Work

There are some basic ground rules which should be followed in setting up group work for school-based assessment in a public examination. A major consideration is that students should fully understand what is required of them.

The teacher should discuss the nature and importance of group work and should elaborate on what is required of students. It should not be assumed that students know and understand this. The discussion with students should help them to understand that their success depends on the efforts of all members of the group. It should also be made clear that completion of an individual assignment will not be accepted in lieu of the group assignment. This is important, since some students who have reservations about group work may assume that they can bypass this requirement by doing an individual assignment.

It should also be made clear that students need to hold themselves and each other accountable for doing high-quality work to achieve the expected outcome. They should be guided about the importance of having meetings either face-to-face or virtually, to complete aspects of the task. They should understand that such meetings are intended not only to share their own ideas but also to assist and encourage others to do so.

Students should know that they need to work out roles and responsibilities to ensure that each member contributes to the work of the group. It should be made clear that each member of the group will be required to work individually outside of group meetings and bring the benefit of such individual work to each group session. At the outset, students should be advised of how and to what extent they would benefit by guidance from and consultation with the teacher to improve the quality of their work.

The size of the group is critical to effective group work. There is general agreement that small groups allow members to participate freely by contributing their ideas and benefiting from critical responses of others and that this conduces to effective learning (Althauser and Matuga 1998). On the other hand, large group sizes often lead to non-participation on the part of some members (Rothwell 2001).

Although group sizes between three and five have been recommended by some researchers (Ngeow 1998), groups of between three and six have been found to be most widely recommended (Bennett, Howe and Truswell 2002). Several factors would affect the size of the group, including the size of the class, but it is recommended that groups be kept small. Therefore, no more than six would seem to be appropriate for group work as part of school-based assessment in a public examination.

The assignment of students to groups is often a matter of concern. Although there is no prescription for comprising a group, the teacher should be cautious about the use of "friendship groups". While these may have the advantage of easy cohesion, the closeness of friendship often leads to the accommodation of certain undesirable behaviours by some members of the group, including social loafing.

Depending on the nature of the assignment, members may be matched in various groups to achieve an appropriate distribution of skills and abilities across groups. Alternatively, students may be randomly assigned to groups. Whatever the approach may be to setting up groups, it is essential that they be comprised in a way that optimizes the prospect of accomplishing the task and its underlying learning objectives.

The teacher should monitor the progress of each group and provide feedback which will serve as positive reinforcement for student learning and progress while pointing to ways in which they may improve their learning and the assignment. In order to facilitate this, the teacher should schedule meetings with groups at critical stages of the assignment to allow them to share their progress.

Where a public examinations board permits group work for school-based assessment, it will normally provide teachers and students with appropriate guidelines for the exercise, including the nature of the task that should be undertaken. A general consideration, however, is that group assignments should be suited to group work. Projects are ideal for the purpose. A project is an assignment which requires students to produce something on an area of work related to a course of study as defined in the syllabus of the public examination. Projects may include preparation of reports or the development of a product or the making of a presentation. Student inputs should be encouraged in defining the details of the project to be undertaken. School-based assessment projects should require students to make use of a variety of higher level skills such as creativity and problem-solving. Whether or not projects are involved, group work can be made more exciting and interesting by setting authentic assessment tasks.

The benefits of pursuing school-based assessment projects as group work bear some relationship to the benefits of project-based learning, and CXC may wish to explore the benefits which may be derived from that approach. This suggestion is made with the full understanding that project-based learning is an approach to instruction and not merely a way of conducting a project that is a practical application of knowledge and skills associated with a part of a programme or assessment. It is a comprehensive model of instruction that organizes learning around projects.

In a paper reviewing the research on project-based learning, Thomas (2000) suggests five criteria which would help to define project-based learning. The first is perhaps the most critical – that is, projects are central, not peripheral, to the curriculum. Thomas emphatically states that "projects *are* the curriculum" (p. 2). The other points made by Thomas may be summarized as follows: (1) projects are focused on questions or problems that drive students to encounter and struggle with the central concepts and principles of a discipline, (2) projects involve students in a constructive investigation – a goal-directed process that involves inquiry, knowledge-building and resolution, (3) projects are student-driven, to a significant degree and (4) projects are realistic, not school-like: they embody characteristics that give a feeling of authenticity to students. In essence, project-based learning is a student-driven, authentic, goal-directed learning experience which involves inquiry, investigation, knowledge-building and issue resolution. Group work may be viewed as a natural fit with project-based learning.

There is an evident relationship between project-based learning and the approach to school-based assessment which is encouraged by CXC. However, for the full benefits of project-based learning to be realized, it will be necessary to reconfigure the requirements of the syllabus to allow students and teachers to use this approach to instruction for the whole of a syllabus or for a well-defined major component of the syllabus – for example, a module in the CAPE syllabus. This is a possible reform which CXC may wish to consider, at least in some subjects, to strengthen the development of invaluable life skills to be derived from project-based learning, which may transcend those currently emphasized in the school-based assessment component of its syllabuses.

Assessment of Group Work

Despite the benefits that can be derived from group work in school-based assessment in a public examination, it can become the vehicle for acrimony, conflict and freeloading and can impose a host of unexpected stress on both students and teachers. While careful planning and implementation of group work is critical to avoiding these pitfalls, assessment of group work is perhaps the area that requires the greatest attention.

Many students, particularly high-performing students, are often fearful of group work because of the view that this will affect their scores and grades negatively. There is, however, some evidence that once the task is completed, students become more comfortable with and support a group grade (Deutsch 1979).

One of the often cited complaints about group work is that it permits inequity of contribution of individuals and results in the unfair award of scores to individuals (Ashraf 2004; Carlsmith and Cooper 2002; Myers et al. 2009). Therefore, assessment procedures for group work must encourage equitable contribution and encourage fairness in the award of scores to group members (Ruel, Bastiaans and Nauta 2003; Strong and Anderson 1990). This can be achieved by using an assessment scheme which provides a reward for members who contribute satisfactorily to the assignment and a penalty for those who contribute little or nothing.

The widespread practice of assigning the same score or grade to all members of a group has generated considerable concerns (Ashraf 2004; Hoffman and Rogelberg 2001). A common score or grade for all group members can often lead to higher marks for students who perform poorly and lower marks for those who perform better, fomenting resistance to group work from high-performing students (Ashraf 2004; Hoffman and Rogelberg 2001; Ruel, Bastiaans and Nauta 2003). The practice of the single score or grade for all members of a group needs to be reconsidered.

One option is to have each student complete one aspect of the task that contributes to the final group product and assess each student on that aspect. While this preserves the individual character of the final score or grade, it is likely to compromise an important principle and benefit of group work – that of interdependence. Those involved in the exercise would be functioning as what Jacques (2001) characterized as a mere collection of people. The expected interdependence would be missing, and the full benefit of group work would not be realized. It is worth noting that social interdependence theory clearly predicts that learning groups will have higher levels of achievement than individuals working individualistically (Bertucci et al. 2010; Deutsch 1962; Johnson and Johnson 1989). These considerations would suggest that this option of having each student complete one aspect of a task that contributes to the final group product and assessing each individually on the completed aspect would negate much of the intended benefit of group work.

A more appropriate option is to divide the marks to be awarded into (1) group scores and (2) individual scores. For example, 80 per cent may be awarded as group marks and 20 per cent as individual marks. Here, students will work collaboratively on the task and make a group submission for which they will each receive the group score (out of eighty percentage points, in this example). The contribution of the individual student to the product will be assessed and an individual score awarded to each student (out of twenty percentage points, in this example).

The individual score may be based on peer assessment of members of the group. Peer assessment may be defined as "an arrangement for learners to consider and specify the level, value, or quality of a product or performance by other equal-status learners" (Topping 2009, 20–21). Peer evaluations have been found to be valid by being highly correlated with teacher ratings (Falchikov and Goldfinch 2000) and supervisor ratings (Conway and Huffcutt 1997). They have also been found to be reliable by providing clear differentiation among members of the group based on their respective contribution (Saito and Fujita 2009).

Peer evaluations may be undertaken by ranking or rating. The ranking approach requires each group member to rank the other members of their group from best to worst (Bushell 2006; Pope 2001, 2005). Alternatively, they may be asked to allocate an established number of points to members of their group, with those contributing the most being awarded the highest number of points and those contributing the least being awarded the least number of points (Carson and Glaser 2010; Maranto and Gresham 1998). The use of such ratings is more appropriate for the award of individual marks for group work.

The rating approach requires each member of the group to rate every other member of that group individually, using predetermined criteria or performance characteristics (Li 2001). Figure 10.1 shows a peer assessment instrument used by the author, which illustrates the type of criteria that may be used. In this case, the peer assessment score awarded to each member of the group would be derived from the average score awarded by the other members of the group.

Anonymity in the peer evaluation is recommended to help in offsetting friendship bias which may derive from the bond formed by members in the group in the process of completing the assignment (Burdett 2007; Saito and Fujita 2009).

CONFIDENTIAL

INDEPENDENT PEER ASSESSMENT

Rate each of the other members of your team on the behaviours below by assigning, for each behaviour, **a score out of 20** *to reflect your opinion of the contribution that the person has made to the group assignment. For confidentiality, please email the completed form directly to the instructor at* _____ *(email address of instructor).*

GROUP NAME/NUMBER. _____

(Insert the group name or number as appropriate)

Behaviours	Initials of Members of the Group (e.g. JM for Jean Major)				
Joins group discussions in a timely manner					
Researches and shares useful information					
Brings useful insights to group work					
Is helpful in working towards a group decision					
Takes on a fair share of responsibility overall					
Total					

Figure 10.1. Illustrative peer assessment instrument

However, based on their findings from a study, Peterson and Peterson (2011) caution that while non-confidential peer assessments may inflate the marks awarded to members of a group, confidentiality may lead to the opposite outcome – that is, the deflation of marks awarded by peers.

A simple resolution might involve teacher mediation of the marks awarded by peers, based on the knowledge acquired by the teacher about each member's contribution. The teacher may make this assessment of the contribution of members while interacting with them as the group works on the school-based assessment task. The teacher may then make the final allocation of marks, taking into account both the peer assessment and his or her own assessment of the student's contribution to the group exercise. This approach would allow for the involvement of students in the award of the marks for the school-based assessment component of the public examination, while retaining the teacher's responsibility for ensuring that the final marks are valid representations of the level of performance of each student.

The Future of Group Work in CXC School-Based Assessment

CXC syllabuses encourage the extensive use of group work, particularly in the case of CAPE. However, the focus of much of the encouragement is on the use of group work as part of the teaching-learning process.

In a few CXC CSEC syllabuses, students are encouraged to undertake their school-based assessment through group work. However, students are required to submit individual assignments for the summative assessment which contributes to their overall scores in the particular subject examination. A few examples will suffice to illustrate this point.

For the school-based assessment assignment in CSEC Economics, CXC (2005a, 27) advises that "students may work individually or in groups to investigate a specific problem. However, each candidate must produce a complete report. No two reports from the same group should be identical." Similarly, for CSEC Principles of Accounts, CXC (2006, 29) advises that "every candidate who enters for the CSEC Principles of Accounts examination must submit a report on a project. Students may work individually or in groups to gather data. However, each candidate must produce a complete report. No two reports from the same group should be identical."

Where group work is permitted in CAPE, a similar expectation is defined. For both units 1 and 2 of CAPE Law, for example, CXC (2010c, 28) advises that "students may work individually or in groups to conduct research. However, each candidate must produce a complete report. No two reports from the same group should be identical." Here, the emphasis is on individual submission of the school-based assessment assignment for individual assessment and the award of individual marks. Despite the pursuit of group work, therefore, no consideration is given to a group mark.

The position taken by CXC might well reflect a concern about possible disproportionate contribution of individuals to a group assignment and the concern that this may result in the unfair award of marks to individuals. However, this approach negates much of the benefits to be derived from group work. The groups working on the CXC school-based assessment function as a mere collection of people (Jacques 2001). The interdependence among group members which leads to higher levels of learning (Bertucci et al. 2010; Deutsch 1962; Johnson and Johnson 1989) is compromised. It seems, therefore, that one of the approaches discussed above for the award of a group mark and an individual mark might well provide a more appropriate approach to the assessment of the school-based assessment task undertaken through group work.

There is some evidence that CXC is beginning to reconsider its position with respect to the assessment of group work undertaken for school-based assessment. In the case of the CAPE Digital Media syllabus, more recently developed, CXC (2013b, 41) advises as follows, for both units 1 and 2: "It is recommended that candidates be provided with the assessment criteria before commencing the project. It is also recommended that students work in groups of 2 to 3 for the School-Based Assessment."

This syllabus does not specifically require the submission of individual pieces, and it was clarified to the author that this is not a requirement for the CAPE Digital Media syllabus (CXC pro-registrar, pers. comm.).

Clearly, CXC needs to embrace more fully the benefits to be derived from group work in providing students with the opportunity for an education fit for their various destinations. It is anticipated that, over the next few years, CXC will give further attention to this matter and that the full benefit of group work will be integrated into the school-based assessment tasks undertaken by groups of students.

11 | A Single Project for Clusters of Subjects

Defining and Using Clusters of Subjects

The use of a single assignment for school-based assessment in clusters of subjects can bring a high degree of realism to the public examination. It can enhance the fitness of purpose of examinations for preparing students for life and for the various destinations to which they proceed, particularly employment. Like group work, which was discussed in chapter 10, it can provide students with the opportunity to develop skills and competencies necessary for success in the workplace and for life in general.

Within the context of a public examination, a cluster may be defined as a group of subjects with a close proximity of relationship to each other by virtue of some common or complementary competencies that they seek to develop. The subjects taken by a student in a public examination may comprise one or more clusters.

A student preparing for the CXC CSEC examination may, for example, pursue subjects comprising a business education cluster. Such a cluster would typically involve any combination, or all, of the following: Office Administration, Principles of Accounts, Principles of Business, Economics, and Electronic Document Preparation and Management. Similarly, a science cluster may include Chemistry, Biology, Physics and Mathematics.

The use of a single school-based assessment for a cluster of subjects can facilitate an understanding and appreciation of the interconnectedness of certain disciplines in the real world. It can also provide a wider scope and improved opportunities for the development and assessment of higher order skills such as creativity and critical thinking. Where students pursue such clusters of subjects, they can undertake a school-based assessment assignment that allows the integration and application of information from various subjects.

The single school-based assessment assignment for a cluster of subjects can provide the well-documented benefits associated with the interdisciplinary approach to curriculum implementation. The interdisciplinary approach is one that requires the conscious application of methodology and language from more than one discipline to examine an issue (Jacobs 1989; Jones 2009). It enriches the overall educational experience. In lauding the importance of the interdisciplinary approach, Jones (2009, 76) commented that "student education has suffered the inferior pedagogy of traditional methodologies that concentrate specifically on only one discipline. The interdisciplinary approach provides many benefits that develop into much needed lifelong learning skills that are essential to a student's future learning." The use of a single assignment for a cluster of subjects in a public examination will achieve these benefits of the interdisciplinary curriculum. It will provide the opportunity for students to pursue a more relevant, less fragmented, and more stimulating experience, help them to break with the more traditional views of the subjects they study, and foster a perspective that will serve them well in the real world (Jones 2009).

The benefits of a single school-based assessment task for a cluster of subjects may be illustrated by the consideration of a possible assignment for a business education cluster.[1] As noted earlier, such a cluster may comprise the following five CXC CSEC subjects: Office Administration, Principles of Accounts, Principles of Business, Economics, and Electronic Document Preparation and Management.

In this cluster, Office Administration is concerned with the study of administrative principles, policies, procedures and technological competencies governing the modern office environment. The Office Administration syllabus seeks to

- provide students with the knowledge, skills, attitudes and competencies to function in the modern office environment;
- develop awareness of the principles, policies, procedures and technological competencies involved in office administration;
- develop technical, planning, organizing, management and problem-solving skills necessary for functioning in a modern office environment;
- provide students with the capability to adapt to changes that impact the business environment;
- help students appreciate the wide range of attitudes, attributes and behaviours necessary for success and advancement in the world of work;
- lay the foundation for career development and further studies in the business field. (CXC 2013d, 1)

This syllabus therefore seeks to provide students with the capability to adapt to changes in a dynamic business environment and to assist in developing their confidence to make the transition from school to the work environment.

Principles of Accounts "provides introduction to the principles and techniques that accountants employ in measuring, processing, evaluating and communicating information about the financial performance and position of a business" (CXC 2006, 1).

The syllabus seeks to

- introduce fundamental principles and practices of accounting;
- develop skills and attitudes useful in a dynamic business environment;
- provide a foundation for further studies in accounting;
- provide an acceptable level of competence for entry-level employment. (CXC 2006, 1)

Here, students are not only introduced to fundamental principles and practices of accounting but also provided with the opportunity to develop skills in applying accounting principles and procedures to business situations.

Principles of Business, the next subject in the cluster, focuses on the theoretical and practical aspects of business activities, which provide a framework to assist in more informed decision-making by individuals as producers or consumers. It provides the opportunity for students to develop critical entrepreneurial and managerial skills needed in the business environment.

The syllabus seeks to

- promote understanding of theories, concepts and practices that are applicable to the culturally diversified economic environment of the Caribbean;
- provide knowledge of business and of its role in a rapidly changing Caribbean and global economic environment;
- provide the opportunity for informed decision-making through the development of skills in critical thinking, problem-solving, research and communication;
- nurture students' creative and entrepreneurial abilities, to enable them to participate fully in the local, regional and global economy;
- sensitize students to the need for responsible social and ethical behaviour in their pursuit of business goals;
- enable students to access and apply appropriate technology in pursuing opportunities and solving problems in business. (CXC 2006, 1–2)

Essentially, Principles of Business provides students with the opportunity to develop the entrepreneurial and managerial skills necessary to prosper in the local, regional or global business environment.

The Economics syllabus introduces students to pertinent concepts and principles of the discipline. It also provides students with critical knowledge and skills that will enable them to communicate ideas using the language and tools of the discipline of economics.

It seeks to

- develop an understanding of the essential concepts and principles of economics;
- equip students with the tools needed for economic analysis, thus enabling sound, informed decisions as consumers of goods and services;
- provide students with the foundation that will enhance their study in other disciplines that include concepts and principles of economics and make use of the analytic approaches of economics;
- develop an awareness and appreciation of economic issues peculiar to the region. (CXC 2005a, 1–2)

Essentially, this syllabus is concerned with the study of how scarce resources are allocated, given the unlimited wants of a society. This subject also seeks to enable students to make better assessment of, and improve their contribution to, discussions on political, economic and social issues.

The syllabus in Electronic Document Preparation and Management takes into account the fact that the computer has become an indispensable tool in the business environment and that the ability to use the computer and critical software is a fundamental skill for prospective employees. It is designed to equip students with appropriate knowledge and skills in the use of relevant hardware and software in the work environment.

The syllabus seeks to

- develop an understanding of the importance of information and communication technology (ICT) in a modern office environment;
- equip students with the requisite skills to assume clerical and administrative roles;
- lay the foundation for career development and advancement in a business environment;
- develop knowledge and skills useful for specialized training in secondary and post-secondary studies and in future careers;
- foster disciplined and ethical behaviours within the work environment;
- develop effective document management capabilities;
- enhance the quality of life and foster personal growth and development. (CXC 2012d, 1–2)

A Single Project for Clusters of Subjects   111

This syllabus emphasizes a number of skills students are expected to possess in a modernized environment, irrespective of the discipline they may wish to pursue or the work environment to which they may wish to proceed.

A school-based assessment assignment may be designed to utilize and integrate competencies associated with all five areas. Such an assignment may, for example, include:

- A Principles of Business aspect of the task, which requires the student to develop a business plan, including the proposed organizational structure.
- An Office Administration section, which requires an explanation of how one of the offices in the organization will operate.
- A Principles of Accounts component, which requires the preparation of illustrative financial statements for the organization.
- An Economics aspect, which deals with the allocation of resources, with special attention to the division of labour and accessing benefits from a financial institution.
- An Electronic Document Preparation and Management aspect, which requires the preparation of relevant documents (including the plan and attachments such as organizational charts and fliers for advertisements) using relevant software and in keeping with acceptable standards of speed and accuracy.

Enhancing the Value of Public Examinations

The use of a single school-based assessment assignment for a cluster of subjects will enhance the value of a public examination. One of the evident benefits is that it will help to avoid duplication in the assessment of skills and competencies students are expected to develop and demonstrate through school-based assessment.

The school-based assessment component of a public examination, such as those offered by CXC at the CSEC and CAPE levels, focuses on the development and assessment of certain specified skills, including practical skills, research skills, interaction skills and motor skills (Broomes 1997). Unnecessary duplication of effort is likely when students are required to undertake a school-based assessment in every subject when these assignments target the same skills in each subject. While this is so for any group of subjects, it is particularly pronounced in groups of cognate subjects which have similar school-based assessment goals.

Moreover, the use of separate school-based assessment assignments for separate subjects, especially for cognate subjects, is likely to promote the artificial compartmentalization of knowledge and skills. On the other hand, the use of a single school-based assessment assignment for a group of subjects is likely to promote a more integrative orientation to the use of knowledge and skills. This will facilitate the development of students' ability to integrate knowledge and skills from various subject disciplines to solve problems or to make informed decisions. A single assignment for a group of subjects will help students to realize that knowledge and skills derived through the study of individual subjects are not isolated chunks and to see the connectivity between knowledge and skills acquired from the study of various disciplines or subjects. This is how students will be required to make use of their knowledge and skills in the real world, particularly the work environment to which most of them will proceed upon completing their secondary and post-secondary education.

This approach of using a single assignment for clusters of subjects will therefore conduce to the creation of the type of graduate we would like to turn out of the education system – that is, one who can function effectively in the real-world environment by integrating knowledge and skills from various disciplines and transferring them to new contexts to resolve existing challenges. In this regard, it is worth reflecting on the words of Shepard (2006), who, in considering the importance of the ability of students to transfer knowledge, posed the following question: "What good is knowledge if it can't be accessed or applied?" Providing the opportunity for students to develop skills of transferring knowledge must be regarded as an important mission of education in preparing students for life. This cannot be easily achieved by the compartmentalization of knowledge and skills. Assignments that require the application of knowledge and skills from different subjects are more likely to bring success in such an endeavour.

Projects are well suited for such assignments. The use of a single project by a public examination in school-based assessment for a number of subjects will facilitate the students' development of critical higher-order skills of assessment, evaluation, reflection, critical thinking, integration, problem-solving and communication, which are important to their future destinations. Such an approach would fit well into the model of using school-based assessment as a way of providing authentic experiences for students, as discussed in chapter 6.

The introduction of project work in Singapore's pre-university curriculum in 2006 (Bryer 2008) was expected to achieve this integration of knowledge and skills across a number of areas. In a conference presentation made at the inception of the project work curriculum, Bryer (2006, 1) explained that project work is "interdisciplinary and requires students to draw knowledge and apply skills from across different subject areas, to reinforce their understanding that these cannot be compartmentalized, or seen in isolation".

Like group work, the single project, properly handled, can reduce the workload of teachers and students. Students, teachers and parents often complain about the school-based assessment requirements of public examinations being burdensome. In relation to the examinations of CXC, Broomes (1997, 160) puts this down to a concern of "managing SBA as part and parcel of the internal work of the school". This might well be a euphemistic statement of the concern, given the continued clamour of students, teachers and parents about the level of demand of the school-based assessment component of the CXC examinations.

The use of a single assignment for a cluster of subjects holds the prospect of reducing the demand of school-based assessment on students and teachers. It would also facilitate the teacher having more time to undertake the formative assessment of the work of students and provide the feedback necessary to guide their progress and improve their learning and performance.

The use of a single assignment for a cluster of subjects will most definitely reduce the workload for the summative assessment of students' work. A teacher who is preparing a class of thirty in three business education subjects may have the unenviable job of marking ninety assignments at the end of the period allowed for completion of the task. If this teacher should be teaching two streams of students, the number of school-based assessment assignments to be summatively assessed may be doubled to one hundred and eighty. Despite the fact that the teacher should be periodically reviewing the progress of students and should therefore be helped in forming a judgement of the quality of the completed work during the process, there is still considerable effort required for the final assessment of the task to ensure the reliable assignment of marks for the finished product and to complete the necessary clerical work to have these marks (and at times, assignments as well) submitted to the public examinations board. This effort can be considerably reduced if a single assignment were to be used for a cluster of subjects.

The way in which the student workload may be reduced by a single school-based assessment task for a cluster of subjects, while engaging in a process that will have a higher degree of realism in relation to the real-world environment, is also worthy of consideration. The circumstances of a student doing five CSEC business subjects, as discussed in the preceding section of this chapter, would illustrate the point. This student would be doing the following five CXC CSEC subjects: Office Administration, Principles of Accounts, Principles of Business, Economics, and Electronic Document Preparation and Management. Under the normal arrangement, this student will be required to undertake five different sets of school-based assessment tasks, one for each subject. If the student were to undertake a single assignment for this cluster of subjects as discussed in the preceding section, not only would the exercise provide a more meaningful and authentic preparation of the student for the work environment and life in general, but it is also likely to have the added advantage of a significant reduction in the workload of the student, compared with undertaking separate assignments for each subject.

The use of a single assignment for a cluster of subjects can also help in the reduction of costs to the student, the school and the examination process as a whole. This will be even more so if the assignment is undertaken as group work, which was discussed in the preceding chapter. Instead of needing to procure items that will facilitate the completion of the assignments for individual subjects, these can be procured for a single assignment which covers the cluster of subjects. This will be particularly evident in the case of certain technical and practical subjects, such as those in the home economics and technology clusters that require students and the school to procure equipment and supplies to demonstrate the required competencies by completing a product.

Challenges

The implementation of a single school-based assessment assignment for a cluster of subjects in a public examination is not without its challenges. Perhaps the most critical challenge is that of defining a task that is suitable for a cluster of subjects. The difference in the content of each subject and the objective of the school-based assessment in developing and enhancing competencies specific to a subject will have to be considered. Can a single task be defined to respond to the expected outcomes of the school-based assessment in all subjects in the cluster? The illustration for the business education cluster, discussed in the previous section of this chapter, suggests that it is possible to define such an assignment. Care will have to be taken to ensure that the demands of the various components of the task make an equitable demand on critical competencies associated with each of the subjects in the cluster. This is a task that could prove challenging for many teachers even with written guidance from the public examinations board. The need for variations of the task, depending on the subjects in the cluster, will require some ingenuity.

A public examinations board may develop these assignments by using expert panels and disseminate them to schools for implementation. However, it may be challenging to cover all combinations of subjects in various clusters. Additionally, such an initiative will detract from the value of school-based assessment in permitting a level of individualization of the curriculum, by allowing teachers and students to define and pursue assignments that take into account their particular interests, which may be linked to the circumstances of their particular school and community.

Perhaps it will be helpful if the examinations board should develop a range of illustrations of school-based assessment tasks covering various combinations of subjects in a cluster. This may be complemented with the training of teachers to develop the expertise for making use of the illustrations in developing their own assignments in keeping with the standards of the board. Additionally, the board will need to provide clear guidance on the number and types of subjects for which such clustering is allowable.

The allocation of marks to the school-based assessment component of the various subjects in a cluster, based on a single assignment, is another matter that will need to be addressed. Would performance on specific parts of the assignment contribute to the school-based assessment marks for each subject in the cluster? Given the integrated nature of the assignment, it may be quite challenging, if not impossible, to allocate marks separately for components of the task associated with each subject in the cluster. One option would be to assign the same marks to the school-based assessment component of each subject in the cluster.

Perhaps even more challenging would be the supervision of the integrated task for a cluster of subjects where the nature of the task requires the expertise of more than one teacher. The larger the number of teachers involved, the more challenging the provision of guidance is likely to be. This will require increased collaboration among teachers of different subjects. Inger (1993), in addressing a related point, noted that "teacher collaboration is a departure from existing norms, and, in most schools, teachers are colleagues in name only. They work out of sight and sound of one another, plan and prepare their lessons and materials alone, and struggle on their own to solve their instructional, curricular, and management problems." The use of a single school-based assessment assignment for a cluster of subjects in a public examination requires a departure from the existing norms. Where a cluster of subjects involves more than one teacher, it will require that teachers from the different subjects collaborate in designing the assignment, as an important precursor to collaborative supervision and assessment of the work of the student undertaking the assignment. This may require an important cultural shift from the way teachers in some schools currently operate – out of sight and sound of one another. Schools which already practice team-teaching will find it less challenging to make the transition to the arrangements necessary for the design and implementation of the single school-based assessment assignment for a cluster of subjects.

What may prove to be a more intractable problem will be the provision of similar opportunities by a public examinations board to out-of-school candidates to pursue a single school-based assessment for a cluster of subjects. The experience of designing the alternative paper to school-based assessment, discussed in chapter 9, should serve as a good foundation for the design of the more comprehensive assignments required for the single assignment for a cluster of subjects taken by such candidates. The challenge of designing these a priori so that they are available as an external paper for the out-of-school candidate will have to be addressed, and so too will the duration of time to complete tasks designed for various combinations of subjects.

Concluding Reflections

The design and implementation of a single school-based assessment for a cluster of subjects has a number of challenges which need to be addressed. The definition of clusters, the design of the assignment and its supervision will represent an innovation for many schools. Many schools may be able to call on the experience of preparing students for integrated subjects, such as social studies, and integrated science, which often involves teams of teachers working together to prepare students for the related public examinations. In these circumstances, teachers often have to work together not only to provide classroom instruction to students but also to design and supervise school-based assessment tasks. The experience of these teachers can form the basis for moving forward and sharing approaches with other teachers who have to work together for the first time, in responding to the need for collaborative work in the design and implementation of a single school-based assessment task for a cluster of subjects.

At the time of writing, CXC was considering the implementation of a single school-based assessment for clusters of related subjects. The writer suggests that careful consideration should be given to the benefits of integrating knowledge and skills from various subjects in defining the school-based assessment task. The challenges which have been discussed in this chapter will also require attention in order to ensure that the single school-based assessment for a cluster of subjects is properly implemented.

Notes

1. This illustration is derived from a paper prepared by Janice Shaw, a graduate student in an internal (school-based) assessment course designed and taught by the author as part of an educational measurement programme.

12 | Adoption of the Benefits of School-Based Assessment through Continuous Assessment

School-Based Assessment and Continuous Assessment

As noted in chapter 4, school-based assessment invariably takes on the characteristics of continuous assessment. In fact, the terms *school-based assessment* and *continuous assessment* are often used synonymously in the literature. Both terms have in common the characteristic of continuous monitoring of students' progress through classroom evaluation. They both represent an alternative or a complement to the assessment of student performance through summative procedures which are associated with the typical external or final examination. However, school-based assessment may be distinguished as the broader of the two concepts. The characteristics of this concept have been the subject of discussion in preceding chapters, especially chapters 4, 5, 6, 7 and 8. The discussion which follows, therefore, focuses more extensively on a clarification of the concept of continuous assessment, which bears a close relationship to the concept of school-based assessment.

The *Handbook on Continuous Assessment of the Federal Ministry of Education in Nigeria*, for example, defines continuous assessment as a mechanism whereby the final grading of a student in the cognitive, affective and psychomotor domains of behaviour takes account, in a systematic way, of all his or her performances during a given period of schooling. This type of assessment is perceived as involving a great variety of modes of evaluation for the purpose of guiding and improving the learning and performance of the student (Federal Ministry of Education 1988). The school-based nature of this assessment is evident. Also evident is its incorporation of both formative and summative assessment.

Du Plessis et al. (2003) outlined seven key characteristics of continuous assessment. These are as follows:

- It is ongoing in the classroom throughout the year.
- It involves many different tasks.
- It is carried out by the teacher.
- It may be developed by the teacher.
- It is marked by the teacher.
- It is used by the teachers to improve teaching.
- It is connected directly to the syllabus being taught.

The distinctive characteristic of continuous assessment is contained in the first of the seven points – that is, it is ongoing in the classroom throughout the year. This is the critical consideration of continuous assessment. It takes place over a longer duration – for example, a school year, as in this instance. Much of what is mentioned for the other six characteristics would define, more generally, the concepts of formative and summative assessment discussed more extensively in chapters 7 and 8.

Airasian (1991) describes continuous assessment as an assessment approach which represents the full range of sources and methods used to gather, interpret and synthesize information about the learner. This information is used to help the teacher to assess student learning at various points in a course of study or programme. Airasian's emphasis is on the formative use of assessment data, through continuous assessment, to aid student learning.

Nitko (2001) describes continuous assessment as an ongoing process of gathering and interpreting information, about students' learning, that is used for making decisions about what to teach and how well students have learned. Here, the emphasis is on the formative use of assessment data from continuous assessment.

However, as noted in chapter 7, Nitko (1994) shared the view that continuous assessment is not entirely formative in nature: it may be either formative or summative. Formative continuous assessment provides the teacher and student with information that guides learning on a day-to-day basis, whereas summative continuous assessment provides teachers, students and other stakeholders with information on how well a student has attained particular targets at various points during the period over which the continuous assessment is undertaken. Like the concept of school-based assessment, which has been explored in earlier chapters of this book, continuous assessment may be viewed as having a formative dimension and a summative dimension. The concepts are clearly related. Depending on the requirements, the school-based assessment of a public examinations board may be undertaken as continuous assessment – that is, as an ongoing exercise over a longer period, such as a school year or a school term.

Consolidating the Benefits

Based on the nature, characteristics and benefits of continuous assessment, it can be of immense value to teaching and learning at all levels of the education system. Essentially, continuous assessment, like the related concept of school-based assessment, can help to optimize student achievement through the use of feedback to improve both teaching and learning.

In the case of continuous assessment, however, students build up incremental credits, through summative assessment undertaken at various points in a defined period, that are used to compute their final summative assessment score or grade. This approach to assessing students is likely to be more motivating to many students, compared with a single summative assessment. It is therefore not surprising that, in the Caribbean, a number of ministries of education have taken steps to embed continuous assessment as an important element of the teaching-learning experience at various stages of the education system.

Continuous assessment facilitates the broadening of the ways in which students can demonstrate what they know and can do. This is a point, well worth noting, that supports the introduction or expansion of continuous assessment in an education system. Continuous assessment, properly used, transcends the mere administration of a series of conventional paper-and-pencil tests. Instead, it provides opportunities to develop and assess the full range of competencies defined in the curriculum. Chapter 6 engages a relevant discussion on this issue.

When Queensland, Australia, abolished external examination, it was replaced by a system of continuous school-based assessment. It was noted that, when this was done, the practice of some teachers of trying to predict what examiners are looking for in the external examination, so as to focus their teaching on those elements, came to an end. It was replaced by a focus, instead, on building up the competencies of students in the areas of study, so as to optimize their learning. The overall achievement of the student in the area of study was based on the cumulative results of the summative continuous assessment undertaken (Queensland Studies Authority 2010).

Continuous assessment encourages good teaching and assessment practices among teachers at all levels of the education system, which aid improved student learning. Where students have to take a public examination which requires a school-based assessment component, this integration of continuous assessment throughout the education system will help both teachers and students to see examination as a natural part of the assessment procedures used in the school system. It will help to alleviate, if not obviate, the improper practices pursued by some schools in implementing school-based assessment and help to allay concerns associated with this type of assessment in a public examination. In view of the benefits of continuous school-based assessment, it is important to consider how the critical elements of this form of assessment may be integrated into teaching and assessment throughout the school system.

Several African countries, including Ghana and Nigeria, have introduced continuous assessment at various levels of their education system. In the Caribbean, this is no less true. Barbados and Trinidad and Tobago are among countries that have already done so. More recently, the Ministry of Education in Jamaica has been moving to introduce continuous school-based assessment as part of end-of-primary-school examinations, currently the Grade Six Achievement Test (GSAT), itself a public examination. These are positive developments that should be encouraged in an education system.

As Maxwell (2004, 6) puts it in summing up the benefits of the continuous school-based assessment used in Queensland, "the opportunities such an approach presents for making assessment serve learning as well as certification, expanding the range of what is learned and assessed, and making assessments more authentic, contextualized and meaningful are very attractive".

Responding to the Challenges

Continuous school-based assessment presents a number of challenges. Its introduction at any level of the education system where it is not currently practised will be met with uncertainty from teachers, students and parents about its value, usefulness and fairness. Consultations with all stakeholders will be necessary to familiarize them with the benefits of this type of assessment and the steps that will be taken to ensure the validity and reliability of the scores awarded to students. The challenges which teachers face with school-based assessment, already discussed in previous chapters, especially chapters 7 and 8, will need to be addressed. In particular, teachers will need to be properly trained in the skill of constructing tasks that are useful and relevant for the curriculum experiences from which students are expected to benefit at particular levels of the education system. They will also have to be trained in developing and using scoring rubrics or mark schemes to assess student progress and accomplishment as well as in using feedback to guide student improvement.

The concern of work overload, about which so many teachers involved in school-based assessment complain, will require attention. The successful implementation of continuous assessment requires that teachers pay close attention to the progress of students, provide the required guidance and feedback for each student and maintain reliable records of student progress and achievement. Teachers generally view these tasks as additional work, and continuous assessment may indeed make greater demands on teachers and require them to take on additional responsibilities. Given that continuous assessment makes greater assessment demands on teachers than a single end-of-term or end-of-year examination, matters such as class size and adequacy of school resources will need to be properly addressed to ensure its satisfactory implementation.

Integrating Continuous Assessment in the School Schedule

Continuous assessment should be an integral part of the teaching-learning process. It has been observed that a few teachers preparing students for the school-based assessment component of CXC examinations, which itself requires continuous formative assessment, have been setting aside periods at the end of the term or the school year, for students to undertake the school-based assessment tasks.

A group of graduate students in a course on internal (school-based) assessment taught by the writer in the 2010–11 academic year undertook interviews with a small sample of teachers in schools in Jamaica to find out how they implemented the school-based assessment requirements of the CXC examinations. They found that 85 per cent of the teachers used the regular class time allocated by the school to provide guidance to students on their school-based assessment tasks during the course of the school year. This is good. They found that 10 per cent of the teachers used only the summer break to work with students on the school-based assessment tasks, while the other 5 per cent did the same thing during the December–January school break. This suggests that desirable practices were widespread and that only a small proportion of teachers deviated from the expected practice. The rest had reduced an exercise which was intended to benefit from formative continuous assessment by teachers to one that was undertaken as a one-shot end-of-term or end-of-year exercise.

Broomes (1997, 160) emphasizes the need to manage school-based assessment as "part and parcel of the internal work of the school". This is equally true of continuous assessment. It is important that teachers set aside time to provide class guidance, group guidance or individual guidance to students undertaking continuous assessment.

Few countries with an education system built on a British heritage have fully replaced the external or internal examination procedures with continuous assessment. However, many are currently employing such assessment as part of the overall assessment of students at one or more levels of the education system. Given that the benefits of continuous assessment are similar to those of school-based assessment, which was the subject of much of the discussion in this book, a more extensive use of continuous assessment throughout the education system has much to offer for the desired improvement of teaching and learning at all levels of the system. Its more extensive use throughout the education system of countries in the Caribbean and elsewhere is worthy of serious consideration.

References

Abdullah, M.H. 2001. *Self-Directed Learning.* Bloomington, IN: ERIC Clearinghouse on Reading, English, and Communication, ED459458.
Agreement Establishing the Caribbean Examinations Council. 1972. Article III (a).
Airasian, P.W. 1991. *Classroom Assessment.* New York: McGraw-Hill.
———. 1997. *Classroom Assessment.* New York: McGraw-Hill.
———. 2001. *Classroom Assessment: Concepts and Applications.* Boston: McGraw-Hill.
AISHE (All Ireland Society for Higher Education). 2006. *AISHE Readings: 2006, Number 1: A Practical Manual for Evaluating Teaching in Higher Education.* http://www.aishe.org/readings/2006-1/eval-summ.html.
Alesandrini, K., and L. Larson. 2002. "Teachers Bridge to Constructivism". *Clearing House: Educational Research, Controversy, and Practices* 75 (3): 118–21.
Althauser, R., and J.M. Matuga. 1998. "On the Pedagogy of Electronic Instruction". In *Electronic Collaborators: Learner Centered Technologies for Literacy, Apprenticeship, and Discourse,* edited by C.J. Bonk and K.S. King, 183–208. Mahwah, NJ: Lawrence Erlbaum.
AERA (American Educational Research Association), APA (American Psychological Association), and NCME (National Council on Measurement in Education). 1999. *Standards for Educational and Psychological Testing.* Washington, DC: AERA/APA/NCME.
———. 2014. *Standards for Educational and Psychological Testing.* Washington, DC: AERA/APA/NCME.
Ashraf, M. 2004. "A Critical Look at the Use of Group Projects as a Pedagogical Tool". *Journal of Education for Business* 79 (4): 213–16.
AQA (Assessment and Quality Alliance). 2003. *Setting the Standard: A Century of Public Examining by AQA and Its Parent Boards.* Manchester: AQA.
Assessment Reform Group. 1999. *Assessment for Learning: Beyond the Black Box.* Cambridge: University of Cambridge.
———. 2002. *Assessment for Learning: 10 Principles; Research-Based Principles to Guide Classroom Practice.* Cambridge: Faculty of Education, University of Cambridge.
Assessment Systems for the Future. 2005. "Aims and Outcomes of the First Year's Work of the Project". http://arg.educ.cam.ac.uk/images/ASF Working Paper Draft 10.pdf. Accessed 20 November 2005.

Beloe, R. 1960. *Secondary Schools Examinations Other Than the GCE: Report of a Committee Appointed by the Secondary School Examinations Council*. London: Her Majesty's Stationery Office.

Bennett C., C. Howe, and E. Truswell. 2002. *Small Group Teaching and Learning in Psychology*. Report and Evaluation Series No. 1. York: LTSN Psychology, University of York.

Berkowitz, D., B. Wolkowitz, R. Fitch, and R. Kopriva. 2000. *The Use of Tests as Part of High-Stakes Decision-Making for Students: A Resource Guide for Educators and Policy-Makers*. Washington, DC: US Department of Education.

Bertucci, A., S. Conte, D.W. Johnson, and R.T. Johnson. (2010). "The Impact of Size of Cooperative Groups on Achievement, Social Support, and Self-Esteem". *Journal of General Psychology* 137 (3): 256–72.

Bissoondoyal, S. (2004). "Assessing Learning: A Commonwealth Overview". In *Commonwealth Education Partnership 2004*, edited by Commonwealth Secretariat, 45–48. London: Commonwealth Secretariat.

Black, P., and D. Wiliam. 1998. *Inside the Black Box: Raising Standards through Classroom Assessment*. London: King's College, University of London.

Black, P. 2004. "Issues in Assessment by Teachers". Paper presented at the seminar Assessment Systems for the Future: The Place of Assessment by Teachers, Cambridge, 12 and 13 January 2004. http://arg.educ.cam.ac.uk/ASF-report1.html#E. Accessed 20 November 2005.

Blake, H.E., and A.W. McPherson. 1975. "Individualized Instruction: Where Are We?" In *Individualized Instruction: Programmes and Materials*, edited by J. Duane, 7–16. Englewood Cliffs, NJ: Educational Technology Publications.

Blatchford, P. 2009. "Class Size". In *Psychology of Classroom Learning: An Encyclopedia*. http://www.classsizeresearch.org.uk/cs%20psychology.pdf.

Bloom, B.S., M.D. Engelhart, E.J. Furst, W.H. Hill, and D.R. Krathwohl. 1956. *Taxonomy of Educational Objectives: The Classification of Educational Goals*. Handbook 1. Cognitive Domain. London: Longman.

Bloom, B.S., J.T. Hastings, and G.F. Madaus. 1971. *Handbook on Formative and Summative Evaluation of Student Learning*. New York: McGraw-Hill.

Bolvin, J.O. 1991. "Individualized School Programs". In *The International Encyclopedia of Curriculum*, edited by A. Lewy, 189–90. New York: Pergamon.

Bourner, J., M. Hughes, and T. Bourner. 2001. "First-Year Undergraduate Experiences of Group Project Work". *Assessment and Evaluation in Higher Education* 26 (1): 19–39.

Bowman, M.L. 1989. "Testing Individual Differences in Ancient China". *American Psychologist* 44: 576–78.

Brenan, R.L., ed. 2006. *Educational Measurement*. 4th ed. New York: American Council on Education and Praeger.

Broomes, D. 1997. *Practices, Problems and Potential of School Based Assessment*. St Michael, Barbados: CXC.

Brown, C.A., M.S. Smith, and M.K. Stein. 1995. "Linking Teacher Support to Enhanced Classroom Instruction". Paper presented at the annual meeting of the American Educational Research Association, New York, April.

Bruce, G. 1969. *Secondary School Examinations*. London: Pergamon.

Bryer, K. 2006. "Pre-University Project Work in Singapore: An Alternative Mode of Assessment in Singapore". Paper presented at the IAEA conference, Singapore, 22 May.

———. 2008. "Assessment and National Educational Goals: The Core Knowledge Skills Subjects in the Pre-University Curriculum in Singapore". Paper presented at the IAEA conference, Singapore, 8 September.

Burdett, J. 2007. "Degrees of Separation: Balancing Intervention and Independence in Group Work Assignments". *Australian Educational Researcher* 34 (1): 55–71.

Bushell, G. 2006. "Moderation of Peer Assessment in Group Projects". *Assessment and Evaluation in Higher Education* 31 (1): 91–108.

Campbell, D.T., and D.W. Fiske. 1959. "Convergent and Discriminant Validation by the Multitrait-multimethod Matrix". *Psychological Bulletin* 56 (2): 81–105.

Campbell, O.A. 2010. "The Adoption of the Mobile Phones in Maintaining Teaching and Learning Quality Assurance in Nigerian Private Universities". *African Higher Education Review* 3: 4–27.

CXC (Caribbean Examinations Council). 1972. The Agreement Establishing the Caribbean Examinations Council.

———. 1974. *Report for the Year 1973–74*. St Michael, Barbados: CXC.

———. 1975. *Information Booklet, November 1975*. St Michael, Barbados: CXC.

———. 1978. *Report for the Year 1978*. St Michael, Barbados: CXC.

———. 1991. *Secondary Education Certificate Regulations*. St Michael, Barbados: CXC.

———. 1995. *The Examination System*. St Michael, Barbados: CXC.

———. 1999. Report on a CXC inter-divisional meeting to review the study "The Shape, Structure and Uses of Caribbean Examinations Council Basic Examinations: With Special Emphasis on the Teaching of English and Mathematics within the Caribbean School System", 2 February.

———. 2002a. *Regulations for the Conduct of the Council's Examinations*. St Michael, Barbados: CXC.

———. 2002b. *School Based Assessment Manual for Principals*. St Michael, Barbados: CXC.

———. 2005a. *Caribbean Secondary Education Certificate: Economics Syllabus*. Kingston: CXC.

———. 2005b. *Associate Degrees*. St Michael, Barbados: CXC.

———. 2006. *Caribbean Secondary Education Certificate: Principles of Accounts Syllabus*. Kingston: CXC.

———. 2007. *Annual Report 2007*. St Michael, Barbados: CXC.

———. 2010a. *Annual Report 2010*. St Michael, Barbados: CXC.

———. 2010b. *Caribbean Advanced Proficiency Examinations: Applied Mathematics Syllabus*. Kingston: CXC.

———. 2010c. *Caribbean Advanced Proficiency Examinations: Law Syllabus*. Kingston: CXC.

———. 2010d. *Caribbean Secondary Education Certificate: Caribbean History Syllabuses*. Kingston: CXC.

———. 2010e. *Caribbean Secondary Education Certificate: Caribbean Social Studies Syllabuses*. Kingston: CXC.

———. 2010f. "CXC and US Universities Sign Articulation Agreements". http://www.cxc.org/node/2354.

———. 2010g. "CXC and UWI Open Campus Sign MOU". *Caribbean Examiner* 8 (1).
———. 2010h. "Internal Assessment Manual for Principals: Caribbean Advanced Proficiency Examinations (CAPE)".
———. 2011. *Caribbean Primary Exit Assessment (CPEA)*. Handbook for Teachers. Kingston: CXC.
———. 2012a. *Caribbean Advanced Proficiency Examinations: Accounting Syllabus*. Kingston: CXC.
———. 2012b. *Caribbean Certificate in Secondary Level Competence: Mathematics Syllabus*. Kingston: CXC.
———. 2012c. *Caribbean Certificate in Secondary Level Competence: Social Studies Syllabus*. Kingston: CXC.
———. 2012d. *Caribbean Secondary Education Certificate: Electronic Document Preparation and Management Syllabus*. Kingston: CXC.
———. 2013a. *Annual Report 2013*. St Michael, Barbados: CXC.
———. 2013b. *Caribbean Advanced Proficiency Examinations: Digital Media Syllabus*. Kingston: CXC.
———. 2013c. *Caribbean Advanced Proficiency Examinations: Management of Business Syllabus*. Kingston: CXC.
———. 2013d. *Caribbean Secondary Education Certificate: Office Administration Syllabus*. Kingston: CXC.
———. 2013e. *Caribbean Secondary Education Certificate: Physics Syllabus*. Kingston: CXC.
———. 2013f. *Guidelines for Candidates Writing Examinations Offered by CXC*. St Michael, Barbados: CXC.
CARICOM Secretariat. 2005. *CARICOM: Our Caribbean Community; An Introduction*. Kingston: Ian Randle.
Carlsmith, K.M., and J. Cooper. 2002. "A Persuasive Example of Collaborative Learning". *Teaching of Psychology* 29 (2): 132–35.
Carson, K.M., and R.E. Glaser. 2010. "Chemistry Is in the News: Assessing Intra-group Peer Review". *Assessment and Evaluation in Higher Education* 35 (4): 381–402.
Chingos, M. 2010. "The Impact of a Universal Class-Size Reduction Policy: Evidence from Florida's Statewide Mandate". Program on Education Policy and Governance Working Paper Series, Harvard University Kennedy School. http://eric.ed.gov/PDFS/ED510250.pdf.
Cipolle, S., J.F. Funston, and C.S. Johnson. 2000. *Portfolio Assessment*. St Paul, MN: EMC/Paradigm.
Cohen, A.S., and J.A. Wollack. 2006. "Validity". In *Educational Measurement*, edited by R.L. Brennan, 355–86. Westport, CT: Praeger.
Cohen, D.K., and H. Hill. 1997. "Instructional Policy and Classroom Performance: The Mathematics Reform in California". Paper presented at the annual meeting of the American Educational Research Association, Chicago, April.
Conway, J.M., and A.I. Huffcutt. 1997. "Psychometric Properties of Multisource Performance Ratings: A Meta-analysis of Subordinate, Supervisor, Peer, and Self-Ratings". *Human Performance* 10 (4): 331–60.
Coppola, B.P. 1996. "Progress in Practice: Exploring the Cooperative and Collaborative Dimensions of Group Learning". *Chemical Educator* 1(1): 3.

Cranton, P. 1996. "Types of Group Learning". In *Learning in Groups: Exploring Fundamental Principles, New Uses, and Emerging Opportunities*, edited by S. Imel, 25–32. San Francisco: Jossey-Bass.

Crocombe, R., and M.T. Crocombe. 1994. *Post Secondary Education in the South Pacific*. London: Commonwealth Secretariat.

Davies, W.M. 2009. "Groupwork as a Form of Assessment: Common Problems and Recommended Solutions". *Higher Education* 58 (4): 563–84.

Deutsch, M. 1962. "Cooperation and Trust: Some Theoretical Notes". In *Nebraska Symposium on Motivation*, edited by M.R. Jones, 275–319. Lincoln, NE: University of Nebraska Press.

———. 1979. "Education and Distributive Justice: Some Reflections on Grading Systems". *American Psychologist* 34 (5): 391–401.

Du Plessis, J., D. Prouty, J. Schubert, M. Habib, and E. St. George. 2003. *Continuous Assessment: A Practical Guide for Teachers*. Washington, DC: American Institutes for Research with support from USAID.

DuBois, P.H. 1966. "A Test-Dominated Society: China, 1115 BC–1905 AD". In *Testing Problems in Perspective: Twenty-Fifth Anniversary Volume of Topical Readings from the Invitational Conference on Testing Problems*, edited by A. Anastasi, 29–36. Washington, DC: American Council on Education.

———. 1970. *A History of Psychological Testing*. Boston: Allyn and Bacon.

Ehrenberg, R.G., D.J. Brewer, A. Gamoran, and J.D. Willms. 2001. "Class Size and Student Achievement". *Psychological Science* 2: 1–29.

Emtage, L. 2003. "Equivalent Routes? A Comparison of SBA Options in CSEC Office Procedures". Paper presented at the CXC/UWI conference Evaluation in Education, Divi South Winds, Barbados, 26–30 May.

Falchikov, N., and J. Goldfinch. 2000. "Student Peer Assessment in Higher Education: A Meta Analysis Comparing Peer and Teacher Marks". *Review of Educational Research* 70 (3): 287–322.

Federal Ministry of Education. 1988. *Handbook on Continuous Assessment*. Lagos: Ministry of Education.

Feldt, L.S., and R.L. Brennan. 1993. "Reliability". In *Educational Measurement*, edited by R.L. Linn, 105–46. Phoenix: Oryx Press.

Fergus, H. 1980. "Some Implications of the Caribbean Examinations Council for the Continuing Education of Teachers". *Caribbean Journal of Education* 8: 322–31.

Francis, J.C. 1981. "Profile Reporting in External Examinations". *Educational Research* 24 (1): 55–61.

Gareis, C.R. 2007. "Reclaiming an Important Teacher Competency: The Lost Art of Formative Assessment". *Journal of Personnel Evaluation in Education* 20: 17–20.

Gibson, J.L., J.M. Ivancevich, J.H. Donnelly Jr, and R. Konopaske. 2006. *Organizations: Behavior, Structure, Processes*. 12th ed. Boston: McGraw-Hill Irwin.

Glaser, R. 1969. "Individual Differences in Learning". Paper presented at the Third Invitational Conference on Elementary Education, Banff, Alberta, 29 October–1 November.

Griffith, S.A. 1999. *The Caribbean Examinations Council: Responding to the Educational Needs of the Region*. Monograph Series 8 on EFA in the Caribbean: Assessment 2000. Kingston: UNESCO.

———. 2000. "Rethinking School Based Assessment". Paper presented at the Inaugural Conference of Caribbean Examining Bodies, Accra Beach Hotel, Barbados, 22–24 March.

———. 2002. "Improving Secondary Education in the Caribbean Region: The Contribution of the Caribbean Examinations Council". In *Secondary Education: A Path toward Human Development*, 213–29. Santiago, Chile: UNESCO.

———. 2003. "School Based Assessment in Public Examinations: A Paradox That Reconciles". Feature address at the Opening Session of the CXC/UWI Conference on Evaluation in Education, Barbados, 26 May.

———. 2004. "The Alternative Paper to School Based Assessment: The Experience of the Caribbean Examinations Council". Paper presented at the 30th Annual Conference of the International Association for Educational Assessment (IAEA), Philadelphia, Pennsylvania, 13 June.

———. 2006. "Where Constructivism Meets Behaviourism: Issues in the Design of a Teacher Education Course in Classroom Assessment". *Caribbean Journal of Education* 28 (2): 144–62.

———. 2008. "A Proposed Model for Assessing Quality of Education". *International Review of Education* 54: 99–112.

———. 2011a. "Centering Assessment for Learning in the Education System: Towards a New Pedagogy for the Caribbean". Paper presented at the Biennial Conference on Education, 15–17 June.

———. 2011b. "Developing an Instrument and Procedures for the Assessment of Practice Teaching: The Experience of a Caribbean Teacher Education Board". *Institute of Education Publication Series*, no. 7.

Griffith, S.A., and Z. Jennings-Craig. 2010. "Study of a Proposed Regional Primary School Exit Examination to Be Developed by the Caribbean Examinations Council". Consultancy Report prepared for CXC, September.

Grima, G. 2003. "School-Based Assessment: Implementation Issues and Practices". Paper presented at the Twenty-First Annual AEAA Conference, Cape Town, South Africa, 25–30 August.

Gronlund, N. 2006. *Assessment of Student Achievement*. Boston: Pearson.

Haertel, E.H. 2006. "Reliability". In *Educational Measurement*, edited by R.L. Brennan, 65–110. Westport, CT: Praeger.

Harlen, W. 2005. "Formative and Summative Assessment: A Harmonious Relationship?". Paper given at the ASF seminar, January 2005. http://arg.educ.cam.ac.uk/images/ASF%20 Report%204%20Appendix%20E.pdf. Accessed 20 November 2005.

Harlen, W., and M. James. 1997. "Assessment and Learning: Differences and Relationships between Formative and Summative Assessment". *Assessment in Education: Principles, Policies and Practice* 4 (3): 365–80.

Heyneman, S.P. 2009. "The Importance of External Examinations in Education". In *Secondary School External Examination Systems – Reliability, Robustness and Resilience*, edited by B. Vlaardingerbroek and N. Taylor, 1–11. New York: Cambria.

Hoffman, J.R., and S.G. Rogelberg. 2001. "All Together Now? College Students' Preferences in Project Group Grading Procedures". *Group Dynamics: Theory, Research and Practice* 5 (1): 33–40.

Hoxby, C.M. 2000. "The Effects of Class Size on Student Achievement: New Evidence from Population Variation". *Quarterly Journal of Economics* 115 (4): 1239–85.

Hu, C.T. 1984. "The Historical Background: Examinations and Control in Pre-modern China". *Comparative Education* 20 (1): 7–26.

Inger, M. 1993. "Teacher Collaboration in Secondary Schools". *CenterFocus* 2 (December). http://ncrve.berkeley.edu/centerfocus/cf2.html.

Jacobs, H. 1989. *Interdisciplinary Curriculum: Design and Implementation*. Alexandria, VA: Association for Supervision and Curriculum Development.

Jacques, D. 2001. *Learning in Groups: A Handbook for Improving Group Work*. London: Kogan Page.

Johnson, D.W., and R.T. Johnson. 1989. *Cooperation and Competition: Theory and Research*. Edina, MN: Interaction Book Company.

———. 2004. *Assessing Students in Groups*. Thousand Oaks, CA: Corwin Press.

Johnson, D., R. Johnson, and K. Smith. 1991. *Cooperative Learning: Increasing College Faculty Instructional Productivity*. ASHE-ERIC Higher Education Report 4, Washington, DC: George Washington University.

Jonassen, D., J. Myers, and A. McKillop. 1996. "From Constructivism to Constructionism: Learning with Hypermedia/Multimedia Rather Than from It." In *Constructivist Learning Environments*, edited by B. Wilson, 93–106. Englewood Cliffs, NJ: Educational Technology.

Jones, C. 2009. "Interdisciplinary Approach: Advantages, Disadvantages, and the Future Benefits of Interdisciplinary Studies". *ESSAI* 7 (Article 26). http://dc.cod.edu/essai/vol7/iss1/26.

Jules, D. 2009. "Concept Paper III: Better Opportunities for the Youth of the Americas: Rethinking Secondary Education in the Caribbean". Paper prepared for the preparatory meeting for the sixth Inter-American Meeting of Ministers of Education, 9–10 July, Washington, DC. http://smartsheep.org/organization-of-american-states-inter-american-council-for-int-v2.

Juwah, C., D. Macfarlane-Dick, B. Matthew, D. Nicol, D. Ross, and B. Smith. 2004. *Enhancing Student Learning through Effective Formative Feedback*. York: Higher Education Academy.

Kivilu, M. 2004. "Politics of Public Examinations in Africa". Paper presented at the Twenty-Second Annual Conference of the Association of Educational Assessment in Africa, Gaborne, Botswana, 13–17 September.

Law, W.K. 2007. "Frontiers for Learner-Centred IS Education". *Journal of Information Systems Education* 18 (3): 313–20.

Lewis, A.C. 1997. "Changing Assessment, Changing Curriculum". *Education Digest* 3: 13–17.

Li, L.K.Y. 2001. "Some Refinements on Peer Assessment of Group Projects". *Assessment and Evaluation in Higher Education* 26 (1): 5–18.

Linn, R.L., ed. 1993. *Educational Measurement*. 3rd ed. New York: American Council on Education and Oryx Press.

Linn, R.L., and N.E. Gronlund. 2000. *Measurement and Assessment in Teaching*. 8th ed. Upper Saddle River, NJ: Merrill.

Macintosh, H.G., and D.E. Hale. 1976. *Assessment and the Secondary School Teacher*. London: Routledge and Kegan Paul.

Maguire, S., and S. Edmondson. 2001. "Student Evaluations and Assessment of Group Projects". *Journal of Geography in Higher Education* 25 (2): 209–17.

Maranto, R., and A. Gresham. 1998. "Using 'World Series Shares' to Fight Free Riding in Group Projects". *PS: Political Science and Politics* 31 (4): 789–91.

Maxwell, G.S. 2004. "Progressive Assessment for Learning and Certification: Some Lessons from School-Based Assessment in Queensland". Paper presented at the Third Conference of the Association of Commonwealth Examination and Assessment Boards, Nadi, Fiji, March.

McLeod, D.B., R.E. Stake, B. Schappelle, M. Mellissinos, and M.J. Gierl. 1996. "Setting the Standards: NCTM's Role in the Reform of Mathematics Education". In *Bold Ventures: U.S. Innovations in Science and Mathematics Education*, vol. 3: *Cases in Mathematics Education*, edited by S.A. Raizen and E.D. Britton, 13–32. Dordrecht, The Netherlands: Kluwer.

Meece, J.L. 2003. "Applying Learner-Centered Principles to Middle School Education". *Theory into Practice* 42 (2): 109–16.

Messick, S. 1993. "Validity". In *Educational Measurement*, edited by R.L. Linn, 13–104. Phoenix: Oryx Press.

Martin, Michela, and Anthony Stella. 2007. "External Quality Assurance in Higher Education: Making Choices". http://unesdoc.unesco.org/images/0015/001520/152045e.pdf.

Miller, E. 2002. "Quality Assurance in Higher Education in the Commonwealth Caribbean". Paper presented at the seminar Higher Education and Science and Technology in Latin America and the Caribbean: Responding to Expansion and Diversification, Fortaleza, Brazil, 8 March.

Ministry of Education [Bahamas]. 2009. "The Examination System in the Bahamas: The Bahamas General Certificate of Secondary Education (BGCSE)". http://www.mypoortal.com/file/MOw/the-examination-system-in-the-bahamas.html.

Mitchell, D.E., and R.E. Mitchell. 1999. *The Impact of California's Class Size Reduction Initiative on Student Achievement: Detailed Findings from Eight School Districts*. Riverside, CA: University of California, California Educational Research Cooperative.

Morrison, R.B. 1974. "The Application of Statistics to Assessment". In *Constructivist Learning Environments*, edited by R.B. Macintosh, 146–56. London: Edward Arnold.

Myers, S.A., N.A. Smith, M.A. Eidsness, L.M. Bogdan, B.A. Zackery, M.R. Thompson, M.E. Schoo, and A.N. Johnson. 2009. "Dealing with Slackers in College Classroom Work Groups". *College Student Journal* 43 (2): 592–98.

Ngeow, K. 1998. *Enhancing Student Thinking through Collaborative Learning*. Bloomington, IN: ERIC Digest, ERIC Clearinghouse on Reading, English and Communication, ED422586.

Nicol, D. 2008. *Transforming Assessment and Feedback: Enhancing Integration and Empowerment in the First Year*. Glasgow: Quality Assurance Agency for Higher Education.

Nitko, A. 2001. *Educational Assessment of Students*. Englewood Cliffs, NJ: Prentice Hall.

———. 1994. "Curriculum-Based Criterion-Referenced Continuous Assessment: A Framework for Concepts and Procedures Using Continuous Assessment for Formative and

Summative Evaluation of Student Learning". Paper presented at the international meeting of the Association for the Study of Educational Evaluation, Pretoria, South Africa, July.

Nunan, D. 2004. *Task-Based Teaching*. Cambridge: Cambridge University Press.

Nye, B.A. 2000. "Do the Disadvantaged Benefit More from Small Classes? Evidence from the Tennessee Class Size Experiment". *American Journal of Education* 109: 1–25.

ofqual (Office of Qualifications and Examinations Regulation – UK). 2013. *GCSE Reform: Equality Analysis Report*. Coventry: ofqual.

OCR (Oxford, Cambridge and RSA). (n.d.). *Reforming GCSEs: The Changing Landscape: A Summary of What's Planned for GCSEs from 2015*. http://www.ocr.org.uk/Images/141803-guide-to-the-gcse-changes.pdf.

Paris, S., T.A. Lawton, J.C. Turner, and J.L. Roth. 1991. "A Developmental Perspective on Standardized Achievement Testing". *Educational Researcher* 20: 12–20.

Peterson, C.H., and N.A. Peterson. 2011. "Impact of Peer Evaluation Confidentiality on Student Marks". *International Journal for the Scholarship of Teaching and Learning* 5 (2): 1–13.

Pond, W.K. 2002. "Twenty-First Century Education and Training: Implications for Quality Assurance". *The Internet and Higher Education* 4: 185–92.

Pope, N. 2001. "An Examination of the Use of Peer Rating for Formative Assessment in the Context of the Theory of Consumption Values". *Assessment and Evaluation in Higher Education* 26 (3): 235–46.

———. 2005. "The Impact of Stress in Self- and Peer Assessment". *Assessment & Evaluation in Higher Education* 30 (1): 51–63.

Popham, W.J. 2001. "Teaching to the Test". *Educational Leadership* 58 (6): 16–20.

Porter, A.C. 2006. "Curriculum Assessment". In *Handbook of Complementary Methods in Education Research*, edited by J.L. Green, G. Camili, and P.B. Elmore, 141–59. Washington, DC: American Educational Research Association.

Queensland Studies Authority. 2010. "School-Based Assessment: The Queensland System". http://www.qsa.qld.edu.au/downloads/approach/school-based_assess_qld_sys.pdf.

Rice, J.K.1999. "The Impact of Class Size on Instructional Strategies and the Use of Time in High School Mathematics and Sciences Courses". *Educational Evaluation and Policy Analysis* 21: 215–29.

Rickford, A.E. 2001. "The Effects of Teacher Education on Reading Improvement". *Reading Improvement* 38 (4): 147–69.

Roach, J. 1971. *Public Examinations in England 1850–1900*. Cambridge: Cambridge University Press.

Robinson, C. 2007. "Awarding Examination Grades: Current Processes and Their Evolution". In *Techniques for Monitoring Comparability of Examination Standards*, edited by P. Newman, J. Baird, H. Goldstein, H. Patrick and P. Tymms, 97–123. London: Qualifications and Curriculum Authority.

Rogers, T.B. 1995. *The Psychological Testing Enterprise: An Introduction*. Pacific Grove, California: Brooks/Cole.

Rothwell, J.D. 2001. *In Mixed Company: Small Group Communication*. Fort Worth: Harcourt Brace.

Ruel, G., N. Bastiaans, and A. Nauta. 2003. "Free Riding and Team Performance in Project Education". *International Journal of Management Education* 3 (1): 26–37.

Saito, H., and T. Fujita. 2009. "Peer-Assessing Peers' Contributions to EFL Group Presentations". *RELC Journal* 40 (2): 149–71.

Salvia, J., J.E. Ysseldyke, and S. Bolt. 2007. *Assessment*. 10th ed. Boston: Houghton Mifflin.

Scriven, M. 1967. "The Methodology of Evaluation". In *Perspectives of Curriculum Evaluation*, edited by R.W. Tyler, R.M. Gagne, and M. Scriven, 39–83. Chicago: Rand McNally.

———. 1991. "Beyond Formative and Summative Evaluation". In *Evaluation and Education: A Quarter Century*, edited by M.W. McLaughlin and E.D.C. Phillips, 16–64. Chicago: University of Chicago Press.

Shepard, L.A. 1995. "Using Assessment to Improve Learning". *Educational Leadership* 52 (5): 38–43.

———. 2006. "Classroom Assessment". In *Educational Measurement*, edited by R.L. Brennan, 623–46. Westport, CT: Praeger.

Skurnik, L. 1976. *The Idea of an Examination*. Eton: Examinations Research.

Slavin, R. 1986. *Using Student Team Learning*. Baltimore: Centre for Research on Elementary and Middle Schools, John Hopkins.

Stephens, C. 2004. "Formative Approaches to Constructing Syllabuses for the Caribbean Advanced Proficiency Examinations". *Caribbean Curriculum* 11: 115–27.

Stiggins, R.J. 2002. "Assessment Crisis: The Absence of Assessment for Learning". *Phi Delta Kappan* 83 (10): 758–65.

———. 2005. "From Formative Assessment to Assessment for Learning: A Path to Success in Standards-Based Schools". *Phi Delta Kappan* 87 (4): 324–28.

Strong, J.T., and R.E. Anderson. 1990. "Free Riding in Group Projects: Control Mechanisms and Preliminary Data". *Journal of Marketing Education* 12 (2): 61–67.

Stufflebeam, D.L. 1983. "The CIPP Model for Program Evaluation". In *Evaluation Models: Viewpoints on Educational and Human Services Evaluation*, edited by G.F. Madaus, M. Scriven, and D.L. Stufflebeam, 117–41. Boston: Kluwer Nijhof.

Sumner, L., and L. Archer. 1996. "Examination Development for Education Reform". Paper presented at the Pan-Commonwealth Workshop, Barbados, May.

Thomas, J.W. 2000. "A Review of Research on Project-Based Learning". San Rafael, CA: Autodesk. http://web.archive.org/web/20030812124529/www.k12reform.org/foundation/pbl/research/.

Topping, K.J. 2009. "Peer Assessment". *Theory into Practice* 48 (1): 20–27.

UK NARIC (UK National Academic Recognition Information Centre). 2014. "Benchmarking the Caribbean Examination Council's Caribbean Certificate of Secondary Level Competence (CCSLC)". Commissioned report prepared for CXC.

UNESCO. 1999. "The EFA 2000 Assessment: Country Reports". http://www.unesco.org/education/wef/countryreports/dominica/rapport_2.html.

Vygotsky, L.S. 1978. *Mind in Society: The Development of Higher Psychological Processes*. Cambridge, MA: Harvard University Press.

Weekes, N. 2013. "Moderating the School Based Assessment Component of the Examination Administered by the Caribbean Examinations Council". PhD diss., University of the West Indies, Cave Hill, Barbados.

Wiggins, G. 1989. "Teaching to the (Authentic) Test". *Educational Leadership* 46 (7): 41–47.

———. 2004. "Assessment as Feedback". http://education.jhu.edu/newhorizons/strategies/topics/Assessment%20Alternatives/.

Wiley, D., and B. Yoon. 1995. "Teacher Reports of Opportunity to Learn: Analyses of the 1993 California Learning Assessment System". *Educational Evaluation and Policy Analysis* 17 (3): 355–70.

Willmott, A.S., and D.L. Nuttall. 1975. *The Reliability of Examinations at 16+*. London: Macmillan.

World Bank Group. 2002a. "Public Examinations System: The Nature of Public Examinations". http://www1.worldbank.org/education/exams/Nature. Accessed 11 December 2005.

———. 2002b. "Public Examinations System: The Nature of Public Examinations". http://www1.worldbank.org/education/exams/Equity. Accessed 11 December 2005.

Index

A

accessibility, and fairness, 74
achievement, as measure of cognitive/
 psychomotor skills, 37–38
Africa
 continuous assessment, 120
 foreign examination boards, 6
Airasian, P.W., 118
Alesandrini, K., 97
alternative papers
 comparison to school-based assessment
  requirements, 88–90
 development challenges, 87–90
 future of, 93–94
 restriction to private candidates, 90–93
 and school-based assessment, 85–87
 validity of, 87
American Educational Research
 Association, 73
American Psychological Association, 73
Antigua and Barbuda, 9
articulation agreements
 CAPE transfer credits, 17–19
assessed curriculum, 60
Assessment and Qualifications Alliance
 (AQA), 34
assessment *for* learning, 69–71, 81
assessment *of* learning, 69–71, 81
assessment practices
 fairness in, 73–75
 measuring achievement, 33–34
 and quality assurance standards, 23–24
 school-based assessment, 40–43
associate degrees (CAPE), areas of study,
  18–19
Association of Commonwealth
 Examination and Assessment
 Boards, 75
Australia
 continuous school-based
  assessment, 119
 examination reforms, 75
authentic assessment, 61–63
 provision of opportunities for, 63–64

B

Bahamas General Certificate of Secondary
 Education (BGCSE), 7
Barbados, 9
 Barbados Secondary School Entrance
  Examination, 21
 continuous assessment, use of, 120
 eastern zone office of CXC, 11
base groups, 96–97
basic proficency, 14–15
 CCSLC as replacement for, 19–20
Belize, 9
Beloe, R., 13
Beloe report, 13
bias, avoidance of in public
 examinations, 74
Biblical examination references, 3

Black, P., 66, 67, 68
Blake, H.E., 48
Blatchford, P., 52
Bloom, B.S., 37
Bolvin, J.O., 47
Brennan, R.L., 61
British examination system
   achievement equivalents, 7
   benchmarking study of CCSLC, 20
   British Civil Service examinations, 4–5
   CSE (Certificate of Secondary Education), 13–14, 41
   eleven-plus examinations, 7–8
   GCE A Level, 16
   GCE O Level, 7, 13, 41
   GCSE (General Certificate of Secondary Education), 41
   influence on Caribbean education programmes, 7–8
   introduction of examinations, 5
   school-based assessment, 40–41
   and within-subject profiles, 34
British Virgin Islands, 9
Broomes, D., 53–54, 112–13, 121
Bruce, G., 3
business education cluster example
   Economics syllabus, 110
   Electronic Document Preparation and Management syllabus, 110–11
   Office Administration syllabus, 108–9
   Principles of Accounts syllabus, 109
   Principles of Business syllabus, 109

C

Campbell, D.T., 39
Campbell, O.A., 23
candidate performance data, in syllabus reviews, 26–27
CAPE (Caribbean Advanced Proficiency Examination), 16
   articulation agreements, 17–19
   associate degrees, 18–19
   authentic assessment opportunities, 63
   external examinations process, and quality assurance, 29–31
   external papers, 57, 58
   grading system, 35–37
   and group work, 104–5
   internal (school-based) assessment, 41–42
   out-of-school candidates, 85
   post-secondary university qualifications, 16, 20
   profile of achievement by modules, 38
   subject units, 16–17
   syllabuses as standards of competencies, 24
   and university course exemptions, 17–19, 38
Caribbean Advanced Proficiency Examination. *See* CAPE (Caribbean Advanced Proficiency Examination)
Caribbean Certificate of Secondary Level Competence. *See* CCSLC (Caribbean Certificate of Secondary Level Competence)
Caribbean education programmes
   and British examination system, 7–8
   Caribbeanization of curriculum, 10
   CVQ (Caribbean vocational qualification), 20–21
   establishment of CXC, 8–10
   international recognition of qualifications, 7–8, 18–19, 20
   national curriculum, quality assurance of, 27
   post-secondary examinations, 16–19
   quality assurance of, 21, 23–24
   secondary level examinations, 13–16, 19–20
Caribbean Examinations Council. *See* CXC (Caribbean Examinations Council)
Caribbean Free Trade Association, and regional cooperation in education, 9, 10
Caribbean Secondary Education Certificate. *See* CSEC (Caribbean Secondary Education Certificate)

Cayman Islands, 9
CCSLC (Caribbean Certificate of Secondary Level Competence), 14
   authentic assessment opportunities, 64
   core requirements, 19–20
   performance scale, 34
   quality assurance arrangements, 31–32
   syllabuses as standards of competencies, 24
   teacher (school-based) assessment, 41–42
   weighting for, 42
A Century of Public Examining by AQA and Its Parent Boards, 34
Certificate of Secondary Education (CSE), introduction of, 13
China, examinations origin, 4–5
civil service testing, 4–5
classroom practices. *See also* teachers
   content-specific pedagogy, 27–28
   fairness of, 73, 75
class size, impact on student learning, 52–53, 120
cognitive/psychomotor skills
   as measure of achievement, 37–38
competencies, standards of, 24–25
constructivist approach to learning, 97–98
continuous assessment, 68–69
   benefits of, 119–20
   characteristics of, 118
   integration of in school schedule, 121
   and school-based assessment, 117–18
cooperative learning, 96–97
cost-effectiveness in delivery of examination services, 6
CPEA (Caribbean Primary Exit Examination), 21
   authentic assessment opportunities, 64
   external papers, 57, 58
   internal (school-based) assessment, 41–42
   and primary school competencies, 24
   quality assurance of primary education system, 32

CSEC (Caribbean Secondary Education Certificate), 13–16
   authentic assessment opportunities, 63
   basic proficiency, 14–15
   cognitive/psychomotor skills as measure of achievement, 37–38
   external examinations process, and quality assurance, 29–31
   external papers, 57, 58
   general proficiency, 14
   grading system, 34–35, 37
   group work, 104
   out-of-school candidates, 85, 86
   syllabuses as standards of competencies, 24
   technical proficiency, 14, 15–16
curriculum
   assessed curriculum, 60
   business education cluster example, 108–11
   design of, and school-based assessment, 61
   enacted curriculum, 60
   individual instruction, and individualization, 48–50, 54–56
   intended curriculum, 60
   learned curriculum, 60
   subject clusters, 107–8
CVQ (Caribbean vocational qualification), 20–21
   school-based assessment, 41–42
   verification of vocational qualifications, 31
CXC (Caribbean Examinations Council)
   administrative arrangements, 10–11
   Caribbeanization of curriculum, 10
   establishment of, 8–10
   examination fees, 11
   examinations as de facto curriculum standard, 27
   external examinations process, and quality assurance, 29–31
   group work in school-based assessment, 104–5

CXC (*continued*)
   Guidelines for Candidates Writing Examinations Offered by CXC, 86–87, 91
   Internal Assessment Manual for Prinicpals, 53–54, 78
   mandate of, 10
   moderation of examination scores, 40, 81
   overseas printing of examination, 6
   primary school examinations, 21
   school-based assessment, 40–43
   school-based assessment guidelines, 53–56, 80–81
   subject clusters, 116
   syllabus development process, 25–27
   syllabuses as standards of quality assurance, 24–25
   teacher training, 27–28
   teacher training workshops, 80
   within-subject profiles, considerations of, 39–40
   zones, 11

D

Dominica, 9
Donnelly, J. H., 95
DuBois, P.H., 4
Du Plessis, J., 118

E

Educational Measurement (Linn), 4, 61
electronic marking, 30
eleven-plus examinations, 7–8
employment sector
   group work as preparation for, 98
   role in syllabus reviews, 26–27
Emtage, L., 92, 93
enacted curriculum, 60
essay papers, 33, 39
examination papers, overseas printing of, 6
examination services, efficient delivery of, 6
examining committees
   analysis of student performance, 31
   role of in external examinations process, 29, 30
external papers, 57, 58
external verifiers, 31

F

fairness, 5
   and alternative papers, 93
   in assessment of group work, 101–3
   in classroom practices, 73
   defined, 73–74
   in public examinations, 5–6, 73–75
   of scores and grades, 78–79
feedback
   concept of, 65–67
   and continuous assessment, 68–69
   in continuous assessment implementation, 120
   as element of quality assurance system, 26
   and formative assessment, 67–68
   formative-summative difference, described, 69, 70
   as positive reinforcement, 100
   principles of good feedback, 66–67
   profile reporting as, 39
Feldt, L.S., 61
Fergus, H., 10
Fiske, D.W., 39
foreign examination boards, costs of, 6
formal learning groups, 96–97
formative assessment
   assessment *for* learning, 69–71, 81
   and continuous assessment, 68–69
   and feedback, 67–68
   of instruction and learning, 50
   teachers' role in, 76–77
formative continuous assessment, 118
formative-summative difference, described, 69, 70

G

GCE A Level, and CAPE examinations, 16
GCE O Level, 7, 13, 41

GCSE (General Certificate of Secondary Education), 41
general proficiency, 14
Gibson, J.L., 95
Glaser, R., 48, 51, 55
Grenada, 9
Griffith, S.A., 25, 27, 68, 69, 92, 93
Grima, G., 42
group work
  assessment of, 101–3
  assignment to groups, 99–100
  confidentiality in peer evaluation, 102–3
  as cooperative learning, 96–97
  group qualities, 95–96
  groups, types of, 96–97
  and group size, 99
  interdependence of members, 101–2
  peer assessment, 102–3
  project-based learning, 100–101
  ranking approach to evaluations, 102–3
  rating approach to evaluations, 102–3
  and school-based assessment, 104–5
  setting up, 98–101
  and student accountability, 99
  teachers as facilitators in, 97–98
  value of, 97–98
Guidelines for Candidates Writing Examinations Offered by CXC, 86–87, 91
Guyana, 9

H

Handbook on Continuous Assessment of the Federal Ministry of Education in Nigeria, 117
Harlen, W., 68–69
Heyneman, S.P., 5
Hu, C.T., 74

I

individualized curricular programmes
  characteristics of, 47
  and CXC guidelines, 53–56
  operational model, elements of, 48–50
informal formative assessment, 67

informal learning groups, 96–97
Inger, M., 115
Inside the Black Box (Black and Wiliam), 67
intended curriculum, 60
internal (school-based) assessment, 41–42
  and authentic assessment opportunities, 63–64
  weighting for, 42
Internal Assessment Manual for Prinicpals (CXC), 53–54, 78
internal verifiers, 31
International General Certificate of Secondary Education (IGCSE), 7
item-teaching vs curriculum-teaching, 59–60
Ivancevich, J.M., 95

J

Jacques, D., 95–96, 102
Jamaica, 9
  continuous assessment, use of, 120
  school-based assessment requirements, implementation of, 121
  syllabus development, 11
  as western zone of CXC, 11
James, M., 68–69
Jennings-Craig, Z., 27
job market
  and CVQ qualifications, 20–21
  and technical proficiency preparation, 16
Johnson, D., 96
Johnson, D.W., 97
Johnson, R., 96
Johnson, R.T., 97
Johnson & Wales University (JWU, US)
  CAPE transfer credits, 17
Jones, C., 108
Jules, D., 27
Juwah, C.D., 66–67

K

Kivilu, M., 6

L

Larson, L., 97
learned curriculum, 60
lettered grades, system of, 34–35, 37

M

market value of CXC, 26
marking centres, 30
marking schemes
    in assessment of group work, 101–3
    and authentic assessment opportunities, 63.–64
    CAPE grading system, 35–37
    CCSLC performance scale, 34
    collation of scores, 30
    CSEC grading system, 34–35, 37
    CXC moderation of marks, 40, 81
    electronic marking, 30
    in external examinations process, 29, 30
    fairness of scores and grades, 78–79
    and grade-awarding procedures, 31
    inadequate feedback from, 66
    as indicators of attainment, 58
    percentage contribution to overall marks, 54
    ranking approach to evaluations, 102–3
    rating approach to evaluations, 102–3
    reliability of, 6, 61
    standardization of, 30
    subject clusters, 114–15
    teacher mediation of peer evaluations, 103
    and within-subject profiles, 34–40
    validity of, 6
Maxwell, G.S., 75, 77, 78, 120
McPherson, A.W., 48
Messick, C., 87
Miller, E., 26, 29
moderation of examination scores, 40, 81
Monroe College (US)
    CAPE transfer credits, 18–19

Montserrat, 9
multiple-choice tests, 33–34, 39
multitrait-multimethod matrix, 39

N

National Academic Recognition Information Centre (UK NARIC)
    benchmarking study of CCSLC, 20
national committees, and CXC, 11
National Council on Measurement in Education, 73
Nitko, A., 68–69, 118
numerical grades
    CAPE system of, 35–37
    CSEC system of, 34–35

O

objective-type tests
    multiple-choice tests, 33–34
    pre-testing of, 29
Oglethorpe University (US)
    CAPE transfer credits, 19
Open Campus of the University of the West Indies
    teacher training, 28
optional papers, provisions for, 55–56
oral examinations, Biblical references, 3
out-of-school candidates
    CXC examination options, 85–87
    guidance of, 88–90
    scores of, 91–93
    as self-directed learners, 91
    and subject clusters, 115

P

parallel examinations, 30
pass or fail examinations, 3
peer assessment, in group work, 102–3
peer learning, 97
Pond, W.K., 26
Popham, W.J., 59
Porter, A.C., 60
post-secondary examinations, 16–19
    matriculation qualifications, 16

primary school
  CPEA measure of competencies, 24
  CXC involvement, 21
private candidates. *See* out-of-school candidates
problem-solving papers, 33
project-based learning
  criteria defining, 100
  and syllabus reform, 101
public acceptance of public examinations, 5–6, 74, 78
public examinations
  administration of, 57–58
  and authentic assessment, 61–63
  authentic assessment opportunities, 63–64
  Chinese legacy of, 4–5
  compromise of, 74
  efficiency in, 6
  in English education system, 5
  external papers, 57, 58
  fairness in, 73–75
  interdisciplinary approach to, 107–8, 111–14
  key requirements of, 5–6
  limitations in assessment of competencies, 57–58
  multiple-choice tests, 33, 34, 39
  out-of-school candidates, 85
  pass or fail examinations, 3
  stress of preparation for, 4
  subject clusters, implementation challenges, 114–16
  subject clusters, value of, 111–14
  teaching to the test, 59–60
  universal design, 74, 80
Public Examinations in England (Roach), 5
public scrutiny, 6

Q

qualifications, international portability of, 7–8
quality assurance
  CVQs, verification of vocational qualifications, 31
  CXC syllabuses as standards for, 24–25
  definitions of, 23–24
  in external examinations process, 29–31
  feedback, as element of, 26
  syllabus development process, 25–27
  and teacher training, 27–28
  at various educational levels, 27

R

ranking approach to evaluations, 102–3
rating approach to evaluations, 102–3
reliability
  of alternative papers, 93
  and fairness, 73
  of multiple-choice tests, 33
  of profile scores, 39
  of public examinations, 5–6
  of school-based assessment tasks, 40
  and validity, 60–61
re-sitting of examinations, 39
Roach, J., *Public Examinations in England*, 5
Robinson, C., 34

S

Saba, CXC examinations in, 10
scheduling of public examinations, 5
school-based assessment
  alternative papers, 85–87
  characteristics of, 40
  and class size, 52–53
  comparison to alternative paper requirements, 88–90
  as component of certifications, 21
  and continuous assessment, 117–18, 121
  and curriculum design, 61
  dual roles of teachers, 75–76
  and group work, 104–5
  history of, 40–41
  individualized curricular programmes, 47–51
  individualizing assignments, 55–56
  internal assessment, 41–42

school-based assessment (*continued*)
  ongoing process assessment, 51
  optional papers, provisions for, 55–56
  percentage contribution to overall marks, 54
  resubmission of assignments, 77
  role of feedback in, 66–67
  single assessment assignments, value of, 111–14
  and student competencies, 59–60
  student progress, assessment of, 49–50
  subject clusters, 108–11, 114–16
  subjects excepted from, 41
  value of in assessment of competencies, 58
Scriven, M., 69–70
secondary education programmes
  CCSLC requirements, 19–20
  CSEC examination schemes, 13–16
  influence of British examination system, 7–8
Secondary Entrance Assessment, 21
Shepard, L.A., 112
shibboleth, as oral examination, 3
Singapore, project work in pre-university curriculum, 112
site visits, 31
Smith, K., 96
social interdependence theory, 102
social variables, impact on student learning, 80
Stake, Robert, 69, 70
stakeholders involvement in syllabus development, 26
Standards for Educational and Psychological Testing, 73
Stephens, C., 25
Stiggins, R.J., 70–71
St Kitts–Nevis–Anguilla, 9
St Lucia, 9
St Maarten, CXC examinations in, 10
St Mary's University (Canada)
  CAPE transfer credits, 17–18
stress of examination preparation, 4

student-ability profiles, 48, 49–50, 55–56
students. *See also* group work
  access to learning resources, 80
  accountability of in group work, 99
  classification of by ability, 5
  as "co-constructors of knowledge", 97–98
  development of practical skills, 62–63
  fairness of scores and grades, 78–79
  feedback on achievement levels, 39, 66
  formative assessment, and feedback, 67–68
  individual differences in student-ability profiles, 48, 49–50, 55–56
  individual focus on, 51–53
  individualized instruction, elements of, 48–50
  stress of examination preparation, 4
  subject clusters, benefits of, 111–14
  syllabuses as standards of competencies, 24
  syllabus review feedback, 26
  teacher guidance of, 51–53, 76–77
  teaching-learning process, as joint enterprise, 70
student-teachers, summative assessment of, 68
St Vincent and the Grenadines, 9
Sub-Committee of the School Examinations Committee (SUBSEC), role in syllabus development, 25–27
subject clusters
  business education cluster example, 108–11
  defined, 107–8, 115
  implementation challenges, 114–16
subject panels
  achievement, skills defining, 37–38
  in development of resource materials, 28
  marking schemes, 29
  role in syllabus development, 25–26
  speciment examination papers, development of, 29

summative assessment, 68–69
   assessment *of* learning, 69–71, 81
   teachers' role in, 77–79
summative continuous assessment, 118
summative-formative difference, described, 69, 70
Suriname, extension of CXC examinations to, 10
syllabus development process, 25–27
syllabuses
   examinations as de facto curriculum standard, 27
   as standards for quality assurance, 24–25
syllabus review procedures, 26–27

T
teacher (school-based) assessment, 41–42
teachers, 80–81
   class size, and quality of instruction, 52–53, 120
   continuous assessment, 68–69, 119
   dual role of, 75–76
   as facilitators in group work, 97–98
   feedback on student achievement, 39, 50
   and formative assessment, 67–68, 76–77
   group work, and teacher workload, 98
   guidance of students in school-based assessment task, 51–53, 76–77
   guidance of through syllabuses, 24, 80–81
   inadequate feedback from, 66
   individual instruction, and individualization, 48–50
   instructional demands of proficiencies, 15
   role in assessment task, 40
   student progress, assessment of, 48, 50
   subject clusters, and workload reduction, 112–13
   subject clusters, implementation challenges, 114–16
   summative assessment role, 77–79
   syllabus review feedback, 26
   teaching-learning process, as joint enterprise, 70
   teaching to the test, 59–60, 62
   team-teaching, 115, 116
teacher training
   in continuous assessment implementation, 120
   and CXC quality assurance, 27–28
   in management of school-based assessment, 53
   Open Campus of the University of the West Indies, 28
   and summative assessment, 68–69
   in summative assessment, 79–81
teaching assistants, 53
teaching-learning process, as joint enterprise, 70
teaching to the test, 59–60, 62
Teaching to the (Authentic) Test, 62
team-teaching, 115, 116
technical proficiency, 14
   job-market orientation of, 15–16
   subjects examined, 16
technical skills, regional demand for, 16
territorial spread, in syllabus panel selection, 25, 26
testing, forms of
   essay papers, 33, 39
   multiple-choice tests, 33–34, 39
   problem-solving papers, 33
Thomas, J.W., 100
transfer credits, and course exemptions, 17–19
Trinidad and Tobago, 9
   continuous assessment, use of, 120
   Secondary Entrance Assessment, 21
Turks and Caicos Islands, 9

U
UNESCO, definition of quality assurance, 23
unfair advantage, in public examinations, 5–6

University of Cambridge Local
    Examinations Syndicate, 7
University of London examinations, 7
university programmes
    post-secondary CAPE qualifications,
        16–19
    transfer credits, and course exemptions,
        17–19, 38
upward mobility through education, 5

V
validity
    of achievement measurements, 39
    of alternative paper, 87
    and fairness, 73
    importance of, 60–61
    and multiple-choice tests, 33
    in public examinations, 5–6
    of test score inferences, 59–60

W
West African Examinations Council, 8
West Indian federation, 11
    origins of Caribbean Examinations
        Council, 8–10
Wigging, G., 62, 65
Wiliam, D., 66, 67
within-subject profiles
    advantages of, 38–39
    assessment and reporting of, 34–40
    cognitive/psychomotor skills as measure
        of achievement, 37–38
    considerations of, 39–40
    grading systems, 34–37
    multitrait-multimethod matrix, 39
    use of by British boards, 34
World Bank Group, 78

www.ingramcontent.com/pod-product-compliance
Lightning Source LLC
Chambersburg PA
CBHW020052200426
43197CB00049B/404